HOW TO FILE FOR DIVORCE IN GEORGIA

with forms

Charles T. Robertson, II
Edward A. Haman
Attorneys at Law

Sphinx® Publishing
A Division of Sourcebooks
Naperville, IL • Clearwater, FL

Third Edition, 1998

Published by: **Sourcebooks, Inc.**™

Naperville Office
P.O. Box 372
Naperville, Illinois 60566
630-961-3900
FAX: 630-961-2168

Clearwater Office
P.O. Box 25
Clearwater, Florida 33757
727-587-0999
FAX: 727-586-5088

Cover Design: Andrew Sardina/Dominique Raccah, Sourcebooks, Inc.
Interior Design and Production: Andrew Sardina, Sourcebooks, Inc.

This publication is designed to provide accurate and authoritative information in regard to the subject matter covered. It is sold with the understanding that the publisher is not engaged in rendering legal, accounting, or other professional service. If legal advice or other expert assistance is required, the services of a competent professional person should be sought.

From a Declaration of Principles Jointly Adopted by a Committee of the
American Bar Association and a Committee of Publishers and Associations

Library of Congress Cataloging-in-Publication Data
Robertson, Charles T.
    How to file for divorce in Georgia : with forms / Charles T.
Robertson, II, Edward A. Haman. —3rd ed.
        p.   cm.
Includes index.
    ISBN 1-57071-376-6 (pbk.)
    1. Divorce—Law and legislation—Georgia—Popular works.
2. Divorce—Law and legislation—Georgia—Forms.   I. Haman Edward
A.   II. Title
KFG100.Z9R63   1998
346.75801'66—dc21   98-12162
                                                              CIP

Printed and bound in the United States of America.
Paperback — 10 9 8 7 6 5 4 3 2

CONTENTS

Using Self-Help Law Books

Whenever you shop for a product or service, you are faced with various levels of quality and price. In deciding what product or service to buy, you make a cost/value analysis on the basis of your willingness to pay and the quality you desire.

When buying a car, you decide whether you want transportation, comfort, status, or sex appeal. Accordingly, you decide among such choices as a Neon, a Lincoln, a Rolls Royce, or a Porsche. Before making a decision, you usually weigh the merits of each option against the cost.

When you get a headache, you can take a pain reliever (such as aspirin) or visit a medical specialist for a neurological examination. Given this choice, most people, of course, take a pain reliever, since it costs only pennies, whereas a medical examination costs hundreds of dollars and takes a lot of time. This is usually a logical choice because rarely is anything more than a pain reliever needed for a headache. But in some cases, a headache may indicate a brain tumor, and failing to see a specialist right away can result in complications. Should everyone with a headache go to a specialist? Of course not, but people treating their own illnesses must realize that they are betting on the basis of their cost/value analysis of the situation, they are taking the most logical option.

The same cost/value analysis must be made in deciding to do one's own legal work. Many legal situations are very straight forward, requiring a simple form and no complicated analysis. Anyone with a little intelligence and a book of instructions can handle the matter without outside help.

But there is always the chance that complications are involved that only an attorney would notice. To simplify the law into a book like this, several legal cases often must be condensed into a single sentence or paragraph. Otherwise, the book would be several hundred pages long and too complicated for most people. However, this simplification necessarily leaves out many details and nuances that would apply to special or unusual situations. Also, there are many ways to interpret most legal questions. Your case may come before a judge who disagrees with the analysis of our authors.

Therefore, in deciding to use a self-help law book and to do your own legal work, you must realize that you are making a cost/value analysis and deciding that the chance your case will not turn out to your satisfaction is outweighed by the money you will save in doing it yourself. Most people handling their own simple legal matters never have a problem, but occasionally people find that it ended up costing them more to have an attorney straighten out the situation than it would have if they had hired an attorney in the beginning. Keep this in mind while handling your case, and be sure to consult an attorney if you feel you might need further guidance.

INTRODUCTION

Going through a divorce is probably one of the most common, and most traumatic, encounters with the legal system. Paying a divorce lawyer can be expensive, and it comes at a time when you are least likely to have extra funds. In a contested divorce case it is not uncommon for the parties to run up legal bills of over $10,000, and horror stories abound of lawyers charging substantial fees with little progress to show for it. This book is designed to enable you to obtain a divorce without hiring a lawyer, and as a practical workbook for paralegals and legal secretaries. Even if you do hire a lawyer, this book will help you to work with him or her more effectively, which can also reduce your legal costs.

This is not a law school course, but a practical guide to get you through "the system" as easily as possible. Legal jargon has nearly been eliminated. For ease of understanding, this book uses the term *spouse* to refer to your husband or wife (whichever applies), and the terms *child* and *children* are used interchangeably.

Please keep in mind that different judges, and courts in different counties, may have their own particular (if not peculiar) procedures and ways of doing things. The Superior Court clerk's office can often tell you if they have any special forms or requirements. Court clerks cannot give legal advice, but they can tell you what their court or judges require. It is a good idea to go by the Superior Court clerk's office, in person, and ask for any particular forms that they require to be included in your divorce paperwork.

The first two chapters of this book will give you an overview of the law and the legal system. Chapters 3, 4, and 5 will help you decide if you want an attorney and if you want a divorce. The remaining chapters will show you what forms you need, how to fill out the forms, and what procedures to follow. You will also find three appendices in the back of the book. Appendix A is a list of the Superior Court clerk's offices, and is arranged alphabetically by county. Appendix B contains selected portions of the Georgia law dealing with property division, alimony, and child support. Although these provisions are discussed in the book, it is sometimes helpful to read the law exactly as the legislature wrote it. Please remember that the law is always changing. Interpretations of these statutes are the responsibility of the courts, and it sometimes happens that, in the interest of fairness, courts subtly (or dramatically) change interpretations of sections of law to conform to social agendas.

Appendix B contains the forms you will complete. You will not need to use all of the forms. This book will assist you in determining which forms you need, depending upon your situation.

Read this entire book before you prepare or file any papers. This will give you the information you need to decide what forms you need and how to fill them out.

Be sure to read "An Introduction to Legal Forms" in chapter 5 before you use any of the forms in this book.

MARRIAGE "INS AND OUTS" 1

Several years (or maybe only months or weeks) ago you made a decision to get married and now you are contemplating a divorce. This chapter will discuss, in a very general way, what you got yourself into, and how you can get yourself out.

CEREMONIAL MARRIAGE

Marriage is frequently referred to as a contract. It is a legal contract, and, for many, it is also a religious contract. This book will deal only with the legal aspects. Prior to most marriages, a license is required. Qualification for the license requires certain blood testing for public health purposes. Once the procedures have been followed, a ceremony is performed. The wedding ceremony involves the bride and groom reciting certain vows, which are actually mutual promises about how they will treat each other. There are also legal papers signed, such as a marriage license and a marriage certificate. These formalities combine to create certain rights and obligations for the husband and wife. Although the focus at the ceremony is on the emotional and romantic aspects of the relationship, the legal reality is that financial and property rights are being created. It is these financial and property rights and obligations which cannot be broken without a legal proceeding.

Marriage will give each of the parties certain rights in property, and it creates certain obligations with respect to the support of any children they have together (or adopt). Unfortunately, most people don't fully realize that these rights and obligations are being created until it comes time for a divorce.

COMMON LAW MARRIAGE

Sometimes there is a question as to whether or not parties are married, and if an informal arrangement conveys the same rights and responsibilities as a ceremonial marriage. The answer in Georgia at one time was "maybe," but since January 1, 1997, the answer is "absolutely not," due to changes in the law. There is a rumor that you can be married as common law simply by living with someone, or dating them exclusively for some period of time, or by having sex with them, or by signing the same name on a motel registry. In fact, some of these elements could be important factors to consider in states with common law marriages, but none automatically mean that you are married.

Technically, to qualify as a marriage relationship only requires three elements:

1. The parties are able to contract,

2. The parties actually do contract, and

3. There is consummation according to law.

These requirements apply equally to common law as well as ceremonial marriages. In a ceremonial marriage, the consummation does not have to be sexual intercourse, but can be the marriage license or participation in the marriage ceremony. A common law marriage usually requires that the parties have sexual relations.

In the absence of a formal ceremony, if there is a controversy about whether a marriage exists, Georgia courts used to look to such circumstantial evidence as continuous living together (the longer they have lived together, the stronger the case for marriage), general reputation, and statements of the parties themselves. Further, if a child is born, the legal relationship may be affirmed in the eyes of the law.

While Georgia still recognizes the common law marriages of other states, Georgia has narrowed the requirements for a true common law marriage and, in the opinion of one commentator, you just about have to go through a ceremony with an unauthorized official to qualify. In any event, an invalid marriage, whether ceremonial or common law, requires no court action for a divorce, but if there is a possibility of a valid marriage, you may want to speak with an attorney and plan to go through a divorce so that there are no problems with any future marriage.

DIVORCE

A divorce is the most common method of terminating or breaking the marriage contract. This procedure is sometimes referred to as a *dissolution of marriage*, or even a *divorce a vinculo matrimonii*. In this book the terms *divorce* and *dissolution of marriage* are used interchangeably, and have the same meaning. In a divorce, the court declares the marriage contract broken, divides the parties' property and debts, decides if either party should receive alimony, and determines the custody, support, and visitation with respect to any children the parties may have.

Traditionally, a divorce could only be granted under certain very specific circumstances, such as for *adultery*, or *mental cruelty*. These were called *fault* grounds and divorce did not happen easily. Fault had to be proven at trial and a simple wish to be single by one party was generally insufficient.

NO-FAULT DIVORCE

Today, a mobile society has demanded easier divorces and Georgia has adopted what is commonly referred to as *no-fault* divorce. A divorce must be granted simply because one or both of the parties want one. The wording used to describe the situation is that "the marriage is irretrievably broken." There simply is no situation in Georgia that prevents any party in a marriage from divorcing if they choose, and their spouse is powerless to prevent the occurrence.

FAULT GROUNDS FOR DIVORCE

There are also still twelve fault grounds for divorce in Georgia:

1. Improper intermarriage. Hereditary diseases are much more likely to appear in marriages between people who are closely related by bloodline. Most societies have forbidden these relationships, and in Georgia, if spouses would be too closely related, they are prohibited from marrying. For the purposes of this book, this applies to such situations as fathers and daughters, uncles and nieces, etc.

2. Mental incapacity at the time of the marriage. Unfortunately, your belief that your spouse has recently lost his or her mind does not qualify for this category of divorce.

3. Impotency at the time of the marriage.

4. Pregnancy of the wife by someone other than the husband, at the time of the marriage, and unknown to the husband.

5. Force, menace, duress, or fraud in obtaining the marriage.

6. Adultery of either party after the marriage. This is especially noteworthy because this ground may prevent the adulterous party from receiving alimony.

7. Wilful desertion continuing for a period of one year.

8. Conviction for an offense of *moral turpitude* which results in a prison conviction of two or more years.

9. Habitual intoxication.

10. Cruel treatment, usually such as the wilful infliction of physical or mental pain upon the complaining party.

11. Incurable mental illness. This category requires some professional certification in practice, and refers to situations in which a spouse is institutionalized, or has been diagnosed as having an incurable mental condition.

12. Habitual drug addiction. While occasional drug use will not go over well with the court, this category does not usually apply to circumstances of infrequent social use of illicit substances. Remember, this category goes both ways. Often one spouse will make a drug allegation, failing to remember the old adage about people who live in glass houses.

There are occasionally very good reasons to allege one or more of these grounds, if true, for strategic purposes. On the other hand, although these grounds may be present in many divorces, most divorces by agreement simply refer to the marriage as being irretrievably broken, a "no-fault" divorce. Making a claim for a "fault" based divorce may require other court procedures, and involve fairly complicated evidence issues. If you are seeking a divorce on any of these grounds you should consult a lawyer.

ANNULMENT

The basic difference between a divorce and an annulment is that a divorce says, "this marriage is broken," and an annulment says, "there never was a marriage." An annulment is more difficult and often more complicated to prove, so it is not used very often. Annulments are only possible in a few circumstances, usually where one party deceived the other, or minors were involved. If you decide that you want an annulment, you should consult an attorney. If you are seeking an annulment for religious reasons and need to go through a church procedure (rather than, or in addition to, a legal procedure), you should consult your priest or minister.

A divorce is generally easier to get than an annulment. This is because all you need to prove to get a divorce is that your marriage is broken. How do you prove this? Simply by saying it. The PETITION FOR DIVORCE (Form 11), reads: "The marriage between the parties is irretrievably broken." That is all you need to do. However, in order to get an annulment you'll need to prove more. This proof will involve introducing various documents into evidence, and having other people come to testify at the court hearing.

GROUNDS FOR ANNULMENT

Annulments are generally only appropriate under one of the following circumstances:

1. One of the parties was too young to get married. In Georgia, both parties must be at least sixteen years old to get married, but must have parental consent if under eighteen. There are a few exceptions, such as if the woman is pregnant or the parties are already biological parents.

2. If one of the parties is guilty of fraud. For example, where one party just got married in order to have the right to inherit from the other, with no intention of ever living together as husband and wife.

3. If one party was under *duress* when he or she got married. Duress means that the person was being threatened, or was under some kind of pressure, so that he or she did not get married voluntarily. Usually, in Georgia, duress refers to substantial threat, such as being at the point of a gun, not simply choosing the lesser of two unpleasant choices.

4. If one party didn't have the mental capacity to get married. This means the person was suffering from mental illness or mental disability (such as being severely retarded), to such an extent that the person didn't understand he or she was getting married; or possibly didn't even understand the concept of marriage.

5. If one party was already married to another person. This might occur if one party married, mistakenly believing his divorce from his previous wife was final. In this era of mobile life-styles, this happens much more often than you think. If your spouse was previously married, a quick check to be sure the divorce is final is not a difficult process to undertake, but you may want to ask your attorney how to go about it, or engage the services of some type of discreet investigator.

6. If the marriage is incestuous. Georgia law prohibits marriage between certain family members, such as brother and sister, aunt and nephew, or uncle and niece.

If your spouse wants to stop an annulment, there are several arguments he or she could make to further complicate the case. This area of the law is not as well defined as divorce. There are Georgia Code Sections outlining the proper procedures to follow, but annulments are much less common than divorces. The annulment procedure can be complicated, and if you believe that it would be the most beneficial process, you should probably consult a lawyer.

LEGAL SEPARATION

Georgia law permits a legal separation, and refers to the process as *separate maintenance*. This procedure is used to divide property and provide child support in cases where the husband and wife live separately, but remain married. This is usually used to break the financial rights and obligations of a couple whose religion does not permit divorce, in situations arising from either mutual agreement to separate or one party's voluntary departure, or to maintain insurance coverage for a separated spouse. It is an old procedure that is gradually fading out. It is possible to obtain support without getting a divorce, but that procedure is beyond the scope of this book.

Fairly recent Georgia law on the subject has made the area of separation agreements even more treacherous ground, as a separation agreement could provide the settlement terms for an eventual divorce. Also, since a divorce is usually inevitable in separate maintenance situations, the process is at least twice as expensive as a divorce alone. If you believe this process is somehow the most appropriate for your circumstances, again you are urged to seek legal counsel.

Do You Really Want a Divorce?

Getting a divorce is one of the most emotionally stressful events in a person's life. Only the death of one's child or spouse creates more stress than a divorce. It will also have an impact on several aspects of your life, and can change your entire life-style.

So, before beginning the divorce process, you need to take some time to think about how it will affect your life. This chapter will help you examine these things, and offer alternatives in the event you want to try to save your relationship. Even if you feel absolutely sure that you want a divorce, you should still read this chapter so you are prepared for what may follow.

Legal Consequences

Dealing with lawyers, clerks, and judges is exhausting, but this is the easiest part of divorce. The stress created here is that of going through a court system procedure, and having to deal with your spouse as you go through it. However, when compared to the other aspects of divorce, the pain of having to deal with the system is not as piercing as the pain of losing a partner and friend. On the other hand, the legal divorce can be the most confrontational and emotionally explosive stage.

There are generally three direct consequences resulting from the legal process:

1. The divorce of two people: Basically, this gives each the legal right to marry someone else.

2.   The division of their property (and responsibility for debts).

3.   The care and custody of their children.

Although it is theoretically possible for the legal divorce to be concluded within a few months, the legalities most often continue for years. This is mostly caused by the emotional aspects leading to battles over the children. For example, a couple divorcing with small children will have to anticipate dealing with each other for nearly two decades. These relationships as ex-spouses routinely extend far longer than the marriage itself.

SOCIAL AND EMOTIONAL EFFECTS

Divorce will have a tremendous impact on your social and emotional lives, and the effect will continue long after you are legally divorced. These will include:

Lack of companionship. Even if your relationship is quite "stormy," you are probably still accustomed to just having your spouse around. You may be able to temporarily put aside your problems, and at least somewhat support each other in times of mutual adversity (such as in dealing with a death in the family, the illness of your child, or storm damage to your home). You may also just feel a little more secure at night, just not being alone in the house. Even if your marriage is one of the most miserable, you may still notice at least a little emptiness, loneliness, or solitude after the divorce. It may not be that you miss your spouse in particular, but just miss another person being around.

Grief. Divorce may be viewed as the death of a marriage, or maybe the funeral ceremony. And like the death of anyone or anything you've been close to, you will feel a sense of loss. This aspect can take you through all of the normal feelings associated with grief, such as guilt, anger, denial, and acceptance. You'll get angry and frustrated over the years you've "wasted." You will blame yourself, your spouse, your parents, and your lawyer for the problems resulting from this unpleasantness. You'll feel guilty because you "failed to make the marriage work." You'll find yourself saying, "I can't believe this is happening to me." And, for months or even years, you'll spend a lot of time thinking about your marriage. It can be extremely difficult to put it all behind you, and to get on with your life.

The single's scene—dating. After your divorce, your social life will change. If you want to avoid solitary evenings before the TV, you'll find yourself trying to get back into the "single's scene." This will probably involve a change in friends, as well as a change in life-style. First, you may find that your current married friends no longer find you, as a single person, fitting in with their circle. Gradually, or even quickly, you may find yourself dropped from their guest list. Now you've got to start making an effort to meet single people at work, going out on the town, and even dating! This experience can be very frightening, tiring, and frustrating after years of being away from this life-style. It can also be very difficult if you have custody of the kids. And the dating scene is (or at least should be) entirely changed with the ever-present threat of AIDS, sexually transmitted diseases, and other communicable diseases.

FINANCIAL CERTAINTIES

The financial changes brought about by divorce can be a very long and drastic adjustment. Divorce has a significant financial impact in just about every case. Many married couples are just able to make ends meet. After getting divorced there are suddenly two rent payments, two electric bills, etc. For the spouse without custody, there is also child support to be paid. For at least one spouse, and often for both, money becomes even tighter than it was before the divorce. Mathematically the costs rise without any increase in income. Also, once you've divided your property, each of you will need to replace the items the other person got to keep. If she got the bedroom furniture and the pots and pans, he will need to buy his own. If he got the TV and the sofa, she will need to buy her own TV and sofa.

CHILDREN AND DIVORCE

The effect of a divorce upon your children, and your relationship with them, can often be the most painful and long-lasting aspect of divorce. Your family life will be permanently changed, as there will no longer be the "family." Even if you remarry, step-parents rarely bring back that same family feeling. Your relationship with your children may become strained as they work through their feelings of blame, guilt, disappointment, and anger. Your children may even need professional counseling. Also, as long as there is child support and visitation involved, you will be forced to have at least some contact with your ex-spouse.

ALTERNATIVES TO DIVORCE

By the time you've purchased this book, and read this far, you have probably already decided that you want a divorce. However, if what you've just read and thought about has changed your mind, or made you want to make a last effort to save your marriage, there are a few things you can try. These are only very basic suggestions. Details, and other suggestions, can be offered by professional marriage counselors.

Talk to your spouse. Choose the right time (not when your spouse is trying to unwind after a day at work, or is trying to quiet a screaming baby), and talk about your problems. Try to establish a few ground rules for the discussion, such as:

☞ Talk about how you feel, instead of making accusations that may start an argument.

☞ Each person listens while the other speaks (no interrupting).

☞ Each person must say something positive about the other, and their relationship.

As you talk you may want to discuss such things as where you'd like your relationship to go, how it has changed since you got married, and what can be done to bring you closer together.

Change your thinking. Many people get divorced because they won't change something about their outlook or their life-style. Then, once they get divorced, they find they've made that same change they resisted for so long.

For example, Cheryl and Henry were unhappy in their marriage. They didn't seem to share the same life-style. Henry felt overburdened with responsibility, and bored. He wanted Cheryl to be more independent and outgoing, to meet new people, to handle the household budget, and to go out with him more often. But Cheryl was more shy and reserved, wasn't confident in her ability to find a job and succeed in the "business world," and preferred to stay at home. Cheryl wanted Henry to give up some of his frequent days golfing "out with the guys," to help with the cooking and laundry, to stop leaving messes for her to clean up, and to stop bothering her about going out all the time. But neither would try change, and eventually all of the "little things" built up into a divorce.

After the divorce, Cheryl was forced to get a job to support herself. Now she's made friends at work, she goes out with them two or three nights a week, she's successful and happy at her job, and she's quite competent at managing her own budget. Henry now has his own apartment, and has to cook his own meals (something he finds he enjoys), and do his own laundry. He's also found it necessary to clean up his own messes and keep the place neat, especially if he's going to entertain guests. Henry has even thought about inviting Cheryl over for dinner and a quiet evening at his place. Cheryl has been thinking about inviting Henry out for a drink after work with her friends.

Both Cheryl and Henry have changed in exactly the way the other had wanted. It's just too bad they didn't make these changes before they got divorced! If you think some change may help, give it a try. You can always go back to a divorce if things don't work out.

Counseling. Counseling is not the same as giving advice. A counselor should not be telling you what to do. A counselor's job is to assist you in figuring out what you really want to do. A counselor's job is mostly to ask questions that will get you thinking.

Actually, just talking things out with your spouse is a form of self-counseling. The only problem is that it's difficult to remain objective and non-judgmental. You both need to be able to calmly analyze what the problems are, and discuss possible solutions.

Very few couples seem to be able to do this successfully, which is why there are professional marriage counselors. As with doctors and lawyers, good marriage counselors are best discovered by word of mouth. You may have friends who can direct you to someone who helped them. You can also check with your family doctor or your clergyman for a referral, or even check the telephone Yellow Pages under "Marriage and Family Counselors" or some similar category. You can see a counselor either alone or with your spouse. It may be a good idea to see a counselor even if you are going through with the divorce.

Another form of counseling is talking to a close friend. Just remember the difference between counseling and advice giving! Don't let your friend tell you what you should do.

Trial Separation. Before going to the time, expense, and trouble of getting a divorce, you and your spouse may want to try just getting away from each other for awhile. This can be as simple as taking separate vacations, or as complex as actually separating into separate households for an indefinite period of time through the legal process of separate maintenance. This may give each of you a chance to think about how you'll like living alone, how important or trivial your problems are, and how you really feel about each other. However, be careful about how you structure this arrangement. There are a number of details to be worked out that parallel a divorce agreement, such as support, custody, and debt payments.

THE LEGAL SYSTEM 2

This chapter will give you a general introduction to the legal system. There are things you need to know in order to obtain a divorce (or help your lawyer get the job done), and to get through any encounter with the legal system with a minimum of stress. These are some of the realities of our system. If you don't learn to accept these realities, you will experience much stress and frustration.

THEORY VS. REALITY

Our legal system is a system of rules and there are basically three types of rules:

1. Rules of Law: such as a law telling a judge how to go about dividing your property.

2. Rules of Procedure: such as requiring court papers to be in a certain form, or filed within a certain time.

3. Rules of Evidence: these require facts to be proven in a certain way.

The theory is that these rules allow each side to present evidence most favorable to that side, and an independent person or persons (the judge or jury) will be able to figure out the truth. Then certain legal principles will be applied to that "truth" which will give a fair resolution of the dispute between the parties. These legal principles are supposed to be relatively unchanging so that we can all know what will happen in any given situation and can plan our lives accordingly. This will provide order and predictability to our society. Any change in the legal principles is supposed to occur slowly, so that the expected behavior in our society is not confused from day to day.

Unfortunately, the system does not really work this way. What follows are only some of the problems in the real legal system:

The system is not perfect. Contrary to how it may seem, legal rules are not made just to complicate the system and confuse everyone. The rules are attempts to make the system as fair and just as possible. They have been developed over several hundred years, and in most cases they do make sense. Unfortunately, our efforts to find fairness and justice have resulted in a complex set of rules. The underlying problem with our system is that it attempts to provide a framework against which all human problems can be addressed, with fairness to all sides. In practice, there are simply too many possibilities in human relationships and the results can sometimes be unsatisfactory. However, keep in mind that on the whole, the system works pretty well.

This is not a game. The legal system affects our lives in important ways, and it is not a game. However, it can be compared to a game in some ways. The rules are designed to apply to all people, in all cases. Sometimes the rules don't seem to give a fair result in a certain situation, but the rules are still followed. Just as a referee can make a bad call, so can a judge. There are also cases where one side wins by cheating. Probably the hardest cases of all are when one side seeks an advantage through unfair actions. I have found those circumstances the most difficult to deal with, and the most expensive for my clients. Disproving the "big lie" can amount to a major undertaking.

Judges do not always follow the rules you think they should follow.
This is a shocking discovery, even for many young lawyers. After spending four years in undergraduate study, three years in law school learning legal theory, countless hours preparing for a hearing, and having all of the law on your side, you find that the judge doesn't appear to pay any attention to your legal theories or law. Judges may make decisions simply on what they think seems fair under the circumstances. This concept is actually being taught in some law schools now. Unfortunately, what "seems fair" to a particular judge may depend upon his personal ideas and philosophy. For example, there is nothing in the divorce laws that gives one parent priority in child custody; however, it is generally conceded that a majority of judges believe that a child is generally better off with its mother, especially if the child is very young. All other things being equal, these judges will find a way to justify awarding custody to the mother. Most judges are well trained, experienced, fine, intelligent, and legally correct. Be aware though that their decisions may be based on procedures or policies of which you are unaware, and the result can make you wonder about their rationality.

The system is often slow. Even lawyers get frustrated at how long it can take to get a case completed (especially if they don't get paid until it's done). Whatever your situation, things will take longer than you expect. Patience is required to get through the system with a minimum of stress. Don't let your impatience or frustration show. No matter what happens, keep calm and be courteous. Be polite: to the judge, to the court clerks, to any lawyers involved, and even to your spouse. However, if you and your spouse can agree on everything, it is possible to complete the divorce process in about thirty-one days.

No two cases are alike. Just because your friend's case went a certain way doesn't mean yours will have the same result. The judge can make a difference, and more often the circumstances will make a difference. Just because your co-worker makes the same income as you and has the same number of children, you can't assume you will be ordered to pay the same amount of child support. There are usually other circumstances your co-worker chooses not to relate, and may not understand.

Half of the people "lose." Remember, there are two sides to every legal issue, and there is usually only one winner. Don't expect to have every detail go your way. If you leave anything to the judge to decide, you can expect to have some things go your spouse's way. It has been said that a perfect compromise leaves both sides a little disappointed. Under the circumstances, prepare to be a little disappointed in any compromise you work out with your spouse.

Justice is not guaranteed. In America, our system gives everyone an opportunity for justice, although we do not realistically have equal financial access to the system. It has proven painfully true to some that you are only guaranteed as much justice as you can afford. This is another reason why trying to work out your individual circumstances is often preferable to leaving your fate in the uncertain hands of the system.

DIVORCE LAW AND PROCEDURE

This section will give you a general overview of the law and procedures involved in getting a divorce. To most people, including lawyers, the law appears very complicated and confusing. Fortunately, many areas of the law can be broken down into simple and logical steps. Divorce is one of those areas.

THE PEOPLE   Law and the legal system are often compared to games, and just like games, it is important to know the players:

The judge. In Georgia, the Superior Court Judge is the single most powerful individual in the county. He has the power to change title to property, assign custody, and in criminal cases, sentence someone to death. Further, in domestic cases, it often requires the majority of justices on the Supreme Court of Georgia to overturn his decisions. It makes sense that you should invest your time in convincing him of the reasonableness of your position. The judge has the power to decide whether you can get divorced, how your property will be divided, which of you will get custody of the children, and how much the other will pay for child support. The judge is the last person you want to make angry with you! In general, judges have large caseloads and like it best when your case can be concluded quickly and without hassle. This means that the more you and your spouse agree upon, and the more complete your paperwork, the better the judge will like it. Most likely, your only direct contact with the judge will be at the final hearing, which may last as little as five minutes. (See chapters 6 and 10 for more about how to deal with the judge.)

The judge's secretary. The judge's secretary sets the hearings for the judge, and can frequently answer many of your questions about the procedure and what the judge would like or require. Once again, you don't want to make an enemy of the secretary. This means that you don't call him often, and don't ask too many questions. A few questions are okay, and you may want to start off saying that you just want to make sure you have everything in order for the judge. Be friendly and courteous, even if the secretary happens to be brusque. He has a large caseload just like the judge, and may be suffering from stress; or he may just be an unpleasant person. However, you'll get farther by being nice than by arguing with him or complaining to him.

The court clerk. Where the secretary usually only works for one judge, the court clerk handles the files for all of the judges. The clerk's office is the central place where all of the court files are kept. The clerk files your court papers and keeps the official records of your divorce. Most people who work in the clerk's office are friendly and helpful. While they can't give you legal advice (such as telling you what to say in your court papers), they can help explain the system and the procedures (such as telling you what type of papers must be filed). Many Georgia courts have mediation processes that are mandatory in the context of domestic actions. Some courts require that the parents in a divorce attend seminars about the effects of the divorce on the children. You should specifically ask the clerk if such programs are in place in your county. The clerk has the power to accept or reject your papers, so you don't want to anger the clerk either. If the clerk tells you to change something in your papers, just change it. Never argue or complain.

Note: Judges, secretaries, and law clerks are generally very patient and conscientious, however, if you anger the judge, his secretary, or the clerk, any one of them can delay your divorce or cause you a number of problems. So be polite, courteous, and friendly to all of these people. It never hurts to engage in a little small talk, or to express your sympathy or understanding for all of the rude people they have to deal with and with their heavy workload.

Lawyers. Lawyers can serve as guides through the legal system. They try to guide their own client, while trying to confuse, manipulate, or out-maneuver their opponent. In dealing with your spouse's lawyer (if he or she has one) try to be polite. You won't get anywhere by being antagonistic or by arguing. Generally the lawyer is just doing his job to try to get the best situation for his client. Some lawyers are truly nasty people, who can't deal with their opponent on a civilized basis. These lawyers simply can't be reasoned with, and you shouldn't try. If your spouse gets one of these lawyers, it may be a good idea for you to get a lawyer also. A lawyer can sometimes get you through the legal system faster, while helping you avoid the "dangers" along the way; just as a wilderness guide can take you faster along the trail, and steer you away from quicksand and dangerous animals. But if the trail is well marked, and there aren't many serious dangers along the way, you may decide not to hire a guide. And so it is with lawyers and divorce. Chapter 3 will provide more information about whether you need a lawyer.

Paralegals. What exactly is a paralegal? Ask fifty people, get fifty answers. The term in Georgia is often used interchangeably with legal assistant, lawyer's assistant, and sometimes, secretary. Basically though, many years ago very accomplished legal secretaries knew as much or more about the system than the attorneys for whom they worked.

These people were given expanded responsibilities in regard to client interaction and dealing with opposing parties. In some states they can even appear in court. In Georgia, their role is severely limited and this is probably due to the non-standard certification process. I have known paralegals with American Bar Association credentials, law school educations, certified paralegal certification, and twenty years experience in the field. I have also met people who called themselves paralegals despite both a lack of experience or even a high school diploma. Usually though, a paralegal in the courthouse or in the employ of an attorney can be expected to be relatively well informed and less expensive than the corresponding attorney, but be careful. The title can easily be abused by individuals with little concern for the responsibilities or the impact of client's lives.

This book. This book will serve as your map of the trail through the legal system. In most cases, the dangers along the way are relatively small. If you start getting lost, or the dangers seem to be getting worse, then you can always hire a lawyer to jump to your aid.

THE LAW   The law relating to divorce, as well as to other areas of social interaction, comes from the *Official Code of Georgia Annotated* (OCGA), published by the Michie Company under contract with the State of Georgia. These are the laws passed by the Georgia Legislature, and are often collectively called *statutes*. This book is designed so that you won't need to look up the law. However, a portion of this law, relating to property division, alimony, and child support, can be found in appendix B.

> **RESIDENCY REQUIREMENT:** One basic law you need to be aware of is that in almost every case, either you or your spouse must live in Georgia for at least six months immediately before filing a petition with the court. If you do not meet the residency requirement, I suggest that you do not invest much time and money going any further.

The other source of law is the past decisions of the Georgia courts. The reason past decisions are important is that the courts deeply value consistency. If some aspect of your case has already been decided by the courts in a certain way, your judge will want to follow that decision. This *case law* is much more difficult to locate and follow than statutes. For most situations the law is clearly spelled out in the statutes, and the past court decisions are not all that important. However, if you wish to learn more about how to find these court decision, see the last section of this chapter, entitled "Legal Research."

THE
PROCEDURE

The law can be very simple in most divorce cases. Whether contested or uncontested, in practice you will need to show the judge the following five things. The only difference between the two types of divorce is how the issues are resolved, and who resolves them. In no particular order the points that must be made are:

☞ Who you are, and that you are in the right court.

☞ When you married, and when you separated.

☞ Why you are entitled to a divorce.

☞ What should be done with your assets and liabilities.

☞ How should custody of your children be apportioned and how should they be supported.

It is a requirement in Georgia that the parties be *legally separated* for thirty days prior to the entry of any final decree of divorce. This usually refers to sexual intimacy, but may also reflect a date long after any sexual relations when one spouse has left the marital residence or begun residing in another area of the house.

Uncontested Divorce. In Georgia, attorneys commonly refer to divorces as being *contested* or *uncontested*. In general, an uncontested divorce refers to a situation in which the parties have worked out all of their differences and are prepared to have their agreed upon terms put into a judge's order. In a contested divorce, some of the issues are not agreed upon by the parties, and the parties are basically presenting their sides of the case to the judge for his decision. His final decision, in either case, is called a FINAL JUDGMENT AND DECREE. The basic uncontested divorce process may be viewed as a five-step process:

1. The parties work out the terms of their divorce, such as child custody and support, alimony, and division of property and debts. While these agreements are generally upheld by the courts, there are some basic guidelines that have to be followed.

2. One party files court papers that have been agreed to by the other party, asking the judge to grant a divorce. These papers are called the PETITION FOR DIVORCE, the AGREEMENT, and may include an AFFIDAVIT REGARDING CUSTODY as well as additional forms.

3. The court must be sure that the other party has proper legal notice of the divorce process and that he or she will be legally bound by the court's decision.

4. A hearing date must be set.

5. On the date of the hearing, whoever was the filing party appears in front of the judge, the evidence is presented, the Agreement is reviewed for formality, and a judgment is issued granting the divorce.

Now we'll look at these steps in a little more detail, and later chapters will tell you how to carry out these steps.

Work out the settlement terms. This may be simple, or impossible, depending on your circumstances. Chapter 5 includes a discussion on how you get an idea of what you have and what you are entitled to, and will discuss property, child support and custody, and alimony and give you a good idea of your exposure.

Petition for Divorce. This is nothing more than a written request for the judge to grant you a divorce and divide your property. A PETITION FOR

DIVORCE form is provided in appendix C of this book, and instructions are provided in later chapters. Once the PETITION FOR DIVORCE is completed, it is filed with the court clerk. You may also hear the PETITION FOR DIVORCE referred to by the older term: *complaint*.

Notifying your spouse. After you've prepared the PETITION FOR DIVORCE you need to officially notify your spouse. Even though your spouse may already know that you are filing for divorce, you still need to have him or her officially notified. This is done by having a copy of your PETITION FOR DIVORCE delivered to your spouse (service of process). This must be done in a certain way, which will be explained in detail later. It can also be done by agreement, and Form 23 in appendix C, entitled ACKNOWLEDGMENT OF SERVICE AND CONSENT TO JURISDICTION, is the more convenient approach if the divorce is by agreement.

Obtaining a hearing date. Once all of your paperwork is in order and has been filed, you need to set a date for a hearing. The hearing date in Georgia must be more than forty-five days after the PETITION FOR DIVORCE is filed, except in certain circumstances by agreement. A hearing is simply a meeting with the judge so that he or she can give you a divorce. This is usually done by contacting the Superior Court Clerk and asking for a hearing date. Sometimes you will be referred directly to the judge's secretary. This can often be done over the telephone.

Attend the hearing. Finally, you go to the hearing. The judge will review the papers you have submitted, and any additional information you have, and will make a decision about whether to grant the divorce, how your property should be divided, who should have custody of your children, and how the children are to be supported. If it applies to your situation, he may also decide whether alimony shall be paid. If you and your spouse agree on these matters, the judge will likely just approve your agreement.

Contested Divorce. Very simply, any case that is not uncontested, is contested. If you and your spouse need assistance with any aspect of the divorce, there is a controversy. Measuring the controversy is part of the lawyer's art of divorce practice. The problem with contested divorces is that often the issues of agreement are so involved, that if the parties are not in total agreement they are effectively in total disagreement. I have heard it said that you can't have a "mostly uncontested divorce," any more than you can be mostly pregnant, it is either one way or the other. If you really have a contested divorce, it may do you well to seriously consider professional assistance, as the intricacies of evidence and procedure are difficult, even for an experienced attorney. It is not illegal to try it yourself...just dangerous, and possibly irreversible.

The steps in a contested divorce have similarities to an uncontested divorce, except that a judge does the "working it out" part, based upon the evidence presented. These steps are as follows:

- One party files papers asking the judge to grant a divorce. These papers are called the PETITION FOR DIVORCE, and may include an AFFIDAVIT REGARDING CUSTODY, as well as additional forms.

- The court must be sure that the other party has proper legal notice of the divorce process and that he or she will be legally bound by the court's decision.

- A temporary hearing date must be set.

- On the date of the temporary hearing, both parties appear in front of the judge, the evidence is presented, and the judge makes the decisions regarding the position of the parties in an abbreviated hearing. A temporary order is issued which applies to such items as who will live where until the divorce is final, who keeps the children, and what support is to be paid.

- If the parties can live with the temporary order, they can make it the final order of the court. If either party does not like the order, they can request a judge or jury trial, called a *final hearing.* This is serious stuff.

Now we will look at these steps in more detail. Keep in mind that this book covers each step in further chapters.

Petition for Divorce. Just like an uncontested divorce, this is nothing more than a written request for the judge to grant you a divorce and divide your property. A PETITION FOR DIVORCE form is provided in appendix C of this book, and full instructions are also provided in later chapters. Once the PETITION FOR DIVORCE is completed, it is taken to the court clerk to be filed.

Notifying your spouse. After you've prepared the PETITION FOR DIVORCE you need to officially notify your spouse. Even though your spouse may already know that you are filing for divorce, you still need to have him or her officially notified. This is done by having a copy of your PETITION FOR DIVORCE delivered to your spouse (this is called *service of process*). In a contested divorce, it is much more likely that you will have service of process than in an uncontested divorce. This must be done in a certain way, which will be explained in detail later. It can also be done by agreement, and Form 23 in appendix C, entitled ACKNOWLEDGMENT OF SERVICE AND CONSENT TO JURISDICTION, remains the more convenient approach even if the divorce is not by agreement.

Obtaining a temporary hearing date. Once all of your paperwork is in order and has been filed, you need to set a date for a hearing. The temporary hearing date in Georgia must be more than ten days from the day the PETITION FOR DIVORCE is served on your spouse, except in certain circumstances. A temporary hearing is usually requested by including a RULE NISI (Form 6) with your PETITION FOR DIVORCE when you file your papers with the Superior Court Clerk. A RULE NISI is simply a form that gets served with your PETITION FOR DIVORCE stating what day the temporary hearing is held. This is rarely accomplished over the phone.

The temporary hearing. Finally, you go to the temporary hearing. The judge will review the papers you have submitted, and any additional evidence both parties present, and make a decision regarding temporary issues, like temporary child support and custody. If it applies to your situation, he may also decide whether temporary alimony shall be paid. You are only allowed one witness at the temporary hearing. Affidavits, if they can be introduced into evidence at all, must be provided to the opposing party at least twenty-four hours before the hearing. Since a temporary hearing may be held in a couple of weeks, and a contested jury trial in a major metropolitan county can be eighteen months, the temporary hearing can be incredibly important. Also your conduct during the time you are waiting for a final hearing could be used against you. Evaluate your personal circumstances carefully before trying this yourself.

The final hearing. If either party is unhappy with the judge's temporary order, the party may request a final hearing. A form for this request is included in appendix C. This generally is requested within six months of the date of the temporary hearing, or the date of the judge's order, whichever is later. The final hearing will be in front of a judge only, unless one party requests a jury. Juries only determine property issues and do not decide custody claims. Most juries are six person juries, rather than the twelve you see on TV. Either the judge or the jury will reach a decision, commonly called a *verdict*. This verdict is incorporated into a FINAL JUDGMENT AND DECREE, which formally destroys the union of the parties.

Mediation. To resolve situations in which some of the terms have not been finalized between the parties, but many areas are resolved, *mediation* may be appropriate. Mediation is a process in which a trained negotiator, working as an independent, is brought in to try and help the parties reach an agreement themselves. This mediation process is mandatory in some counties, and many courts offer the procedure as *alternative dispute resolution*. As this process is evolving, it may be appropriate to ask your Superior Court Clerk if there is a list of approved domestic mediators for your county, and talk to that office about the procedure as it relates to your circumstances. The cost of mediation (which can range from about $250 to over $1,500), is usually shared by the parties. In many metro Atlanta counties, mediation is now a requirement, so be sure to check with the court clerk.

The judge can order the husband and wife into mediation when the parties are having a difficult time reaching agreement on the major issues. Also, marriage counseling can be ordered if the judge has reason to believe that the marriage can be saved; however, marriage counseling ordered by the court is an unlikely scenario...don't count on it. The judge can also direct either the state Department of Family and Children's Services, or appoint a guardian ad litem, to investigate the circumstances of the parties and provide the judge with a custody recommendation. A guardian ad litem is most often another independent attorney, for whose services the parties are responsible for paying. If one is appointed, it is crucial that you cooperate with him or her whenever possible. Their reports seem to be considered very strongly by the judge.

LEGAL RESEARCH

This book is not a course in legal research, and for most simple cases, you don't need to do legal research. However, if your case becomes complicated, or you simply have an interest in checking into the divorce law in Georgia, this section will give you some basic guidance.

OFFICIAL CODE OF GEORGIA ANNOTATED

The main source of information on Georgia divorce law is the *Official Code of Georgia Annotated* (OCGA). These are numerous volumes that contain the laws passed by the Georgia Legislature. Each section is followed by summaries (called *annotations*) that discuss that section. For example, if you are looking for information about temporary alimony, you would find section 19-6-3. This would give you the exact language of the statute, which would be followed by summaries of court opinions explaining the temporary alimony statute.

These volumes are supplemented as needed. It is important to note that in the backs of some of the books will be paper inserts which comprise the latest legislative activity on a particular area. It is essential to look both in the main text of the book, and in the back section, to make sure there haven't been any changes since the last publication of that volume. A set can usually be found at the public library, although check to be sure they have the most recent set. You will primarily be concerned with Chapter 19 of the Georgia Code, although you can look for other subjects in the index volume.

In addition to the laws passed by the legislature, law is also made by the decisions of the judges in various cases each year. To find this *case law* you will need to go to a law library. Each county has a law library connected with the court, so you can ask the court clerk where the library is located. Be aware that one or two law libraries with which I have been acquainted did not encourage casual research by untrained individuals, so govern your own actions accordingly. Law schools have libraries that may be open to the public. Don't be afraid to ask the librarian for assistance. They cannot give you legal advice, but they can tell you where the books are located and they might even be kind enough to give you a short course on legal research. In addition to OCGA, there are several types of books used to find the case law:

GEORGIA DIGEST
The *Georgia Digest* is a set of volumes which give short summaries of cases, and the place where you can find the court's full written opinion. The information in the *Georgia Digest* is arranged alphabetically by subject. Look first in the index (a four volume set divided by alphabet), find the heading for "Divorce," then look for the specific subject area you want to investigate.

SOUTHEASTERN REPORTER
The *Southeastern Reporter* is a large set of books where the appeals courts publish their written opinions on the cases they hear. There are two "series" of the *Southeastern Reporter*, the older cases being found in the *Southeaster Reporter* (abbreviated "S.E."), and newer cases being found in the *Southeastern Reporter 2d Series* (abbreviated "S.E.2d"). For example, if the digest tells you that the case of *Smith v. Smith* is located

at "349 S.E.2d 721 (1991)," you can find the case by going to Volume 349 of the *Southeastern Reporter 2d Series*, and turning to page 721. In its opinion (which was printed in 1991), the court will discuss what the case was about, what questions of law were presented for consideration, and what the court decided and why.

UNIFORM
SUPERIOR
COURT RULES

The *Uniform Superior Court Rules* are the rules that are applied in the various courts in Georgia, and they also contain approved forms. These rules mainly deal with forms and procedures. You would be primarily concerned with the "Rules of Civil Procedure."

OTHER
SOURCES

Four books you may want to ask for at the law library are:

☛ *Georgia Divorce, Alimony and Child Custody*, by the Harrison Company.

☛ *Georgia Family Law*, by Abrams (published by Matthew-Bender).

☛ *Georgia Dissolution of Marriage*, by the Georgia Bar Continuing Legal Education.

☛ *Georgia Civil Trial Practice*, by the Georgia Bar Continuing Legal Education.

You may find other books on divorce law also.

LAWYERS 3

Georgia courts do not generally require an attorney to represent you. A party in Georgia has a constitutional right to represent his or herself. Whether you need an attorney will depend upon many factors, such as how comfortable you feel handling the matter yourself, whether your situation is more complicated than usual, how much opposition you get from your spouse, and whether your spouse has an attorney. It may also be advisable to hire an attorney if you encounter a judge with a hostile attitude, or if your spouse gets a lawyer who wants to fight. There are no court appointed lawyers in divorce cases, so if you want an attorney you will have to hire one. It is also against the law in Georgia for an attorney to handle a divorce case on a *contingency fee* basis, so be prepared to discuss money fairly early in the conversation.

A very general rule is that you should consider hiring an attorney whenever you reach a point where you no longer feel comfortable representing yourself. This point will vary greatly with each person, so there is no easy way to be more definite. The cases in which attorneys are rarely required are marriages of very short duration, which resulted in neither children, nor substantial possessions, and which was not further complicated by many assets or liabilities. In cases where your spouse refuses to come to some agreement, retirement benefits or tax complications exist, or custody is challenged, attorneys are inevitable.

Rather than asking if you *need* a lawyer, a more appropriate question is: Do you *want* a lawyer? The next section will discuss some of the *pros* and *cons* of hiring a lawyer, and some of the things you may want to consider in making this decision.

DO YOU WANT A LAWYER?

One of the first questions you will want to consider, and most likely the reason you are reading this book, is: How much will an attorney cost? Attorneys come in all ages, shapes, sizes, sexes, racial and ethnic groups—and price ranges. For a very rough estimate, you can expect an attorney to charge anywhere from $80 to $1,500 total for an uncontested divorce, and from $1,500 and up (for each of you) for a contested divorce. Lawyers usually charge an hourly rate for contested divorces, ranging from about $75 to $300 per hour. Most new (and often less expensive) attorneys would be quite capable of handling a simple divorce, but, if your situation became more complicated, you would probably prefer a more experienced lawyer.

ADVANTAGES TO HAVING A LAWYER

The following are some of the advantages to hiring a lawyer:

☛ Judges and other attorneys may take you more seriously. Most judges prefer both parties to have attorneys. They feel this helps the case move in a more orderly fashion, because both sides will know the procedures and relevant issues. Persons representing themselves very often waste a lot of time on matters that have absolutely no bearing on the outcome of the case.

☛ A lawyer will serve as a "buffer" between you and your spouse. This can lead to a quicker passage through the system, by reducing the chance for emotions to take control and confuse the issues.

☛ Attorneys often prefer to deal with other attorneys, for the same reasons listed above. However, if you become familiar with this book, and conduct yourself in a calm and proper manner, you should have no trouble. (Proper courtroom manners will be discussed in chapter 5.)

☞ You can let your lawyer worry about all of the details. By having an attorney you need only to become generally familiar with the contents of this book. As it will be your attorney's job to file the proper papers in the correct form, and to deal with the court clerks, the judge, the process server, your spouse, and your spouse's attorney.

☞ Lawyers provide professional assistance with problems. In the event your case is complicated, or suddenly becomes complicated, it is an advantage to have an attorney who is familiar with your case. It can also be comforting to have a lawyer to turn to for advice, and to get your questions answered.

ADVANTAGES TO
REPRESENTING
YOURSELF

There are also significant advantages to representing yourself:

☞ You save the cost of a lawyer.

☞ Sometimes judges feel more sympathetic toward a person not represented by an attorney. Sometimes this results in the unrepresented person being allowed a certain amount of leeway with the procedure rules.

☞ The procedure may be faster. Two of the most frequent complaints about lawyers received by the bar association involve delay in completing the case, and failure to return phone calls. Most lawyers have a heavy caseload, which sometimes results in cases being neglected for various periods of time. If you are following the progress of your own case you'll be able to push it along the system diligently.

☞ Selecting an attorney is not easy. As the next section shows, it is hard to know whether you will be happy with the attorney you select.

MIDDLE
GROUND

You may want to look for an attorney who will be willing to accept an hourly fee to answer your questions and give you help as you need it. This way you will save some legal costs, but still get some professional assistance. For malpractice purposes, many attorneys may be reluctant to accept this arrangement unless it is outlined in detail (and at your expense) in an agreement between the two of you.

There are also non-legal avenues of assistance available, such as "We The People" franchises designed to assist with the filing of forms. Further, some paralegal companies have been formed that offer assistance in these matters. As a paralegal myself for several years, I caution you that the state rules for paralegals acting independently of lawyers are on very shaky ground. While a paralegal may provide you with a certain level of legal information to assist in filing your forms, he or she cannot provide any legal advice, nor appear in court on your behalf. Although I sympathize with the current problems of getting good legal services to the people at a reasonable price, and know many paralegals who are as well informed as I on the subject, it is still against the law in Georgia to engage in, or assist anyone else in engaging in, the unauthorized practice of law.

It is also possible for both you and your spouse to hire one attorney. However, ***be careful***. This arrangement is not favored in Georgia, and the attorney will only be able to represent one of you (or neither of you) and will require you to sign lots of releases explaining that you understand that one attorney cannot represent two people in a divorce. However, if the case is uncontested, and you simply want the attorney to draft the documents, it is possible to use only one attorney.

SELECTING A LAWYER

Selecting a lawyer is a two-step process. First you need to decide which attorney to make an appointment with, then you need to decide if you want to hire that attorney.

FINDING
LAWYERS

The following suggestions may help you locate a few lawyers for further consideration:

☛ *Ask a friend.* A common, and frequently the best, way to find a lawyer is to ask someone you know to recommend one to you. This is especially helpful if the lawyer represented your friend in a divorce, or other family law matter.

☛ *Lawyer referral service.* You can find a referral service by looking in the Yellow Pages phone directory under "Attorney Referral Services" or "Attorneys." This is a service, usually operated by a bar association, which is designed to match a client with an attorney handling cases in the area of law the client needs. The referral service does not guarantee the quality of work, nor the level of experience or ability, of the attorney. Finding a lawyer this way will at least connect you with one who is interested in divorce and family law matters, and probably has some experience in this area.

☛ *Yellow Pages.* Check under the heading for "Attorneys" in the Yellow Pages phone directory. Many of the lawyers and law firms will place display ads here indicating their areas of practice, and educational backgrounds. Look for firms or lawyers which indicate they practice in areas such as "divorce," "family law," or "domestic relations."

☛ *Ask another lawyer.* If you have used the services of an attorney in the past for some other matter (for example, a real estate closing, traffic ticket, or a will), you may want to call and ask if he or she could refer you to an attorney whose ability in the area of family law is respected.

☛ Look for signs in your neighborhood shopping district, or on your way to and from work. Attorneys who practice in your area of town are probably very familiar with the economics of the community, and are often familiar with general practice issues like simple divorces.

☞ Look in the phone book for your local county or state "bar" association. Call them and ask for a referral to a member of a domestic relations or family law practice section committee. This is routinely provided as a low cost or free service by bar associations.

☞ Check the Internet, if you are computer literate. Many domestic attorneys have Web pages, many firms are listed, and most major on-line services have extensive domestic relations sections. I have volunteered for over a year on *America Online*, for example, which has a section called the "Legal Pad."

EVALUATING A
LAWYER

From your search you should select three to five lawyers worthy of further consideration. Your first step will be to call each attorney's office, explain that you are interested in seeking a divorce, and ask the following questions:

☞ Does the attorney (or firm) handle this type of matter?

☞ How much can you expect it to cost? (Don't expect to get much of a definite answer, but you should be able obtain an hourly rate, a range of total cost for a simple case, and information about what variables might increase the costs. However, you may need to discuss this with the attorney, rather than the person answering the phone at the attorney's office.)

☞ How soon can you get an appointment?

If you like the answers you get, ask if you can speak to the attorney. Some offices will permit this, but others will require you to make an appointment. Make the appointment if that is what is required. Once you get in contact with the attorney (either on the phone or at the appointment), ask the following questions:

☞ How much will it cost?

☞ How will the fee be paid? (Many attorneys will accept credit cards, or promissory notes secured by property in which you have personal equity. It never hurts to ask.)

☞ Can you see a copy of his standard fee agreement or letter?

☞ How long has the attorney been in practice?

☞ How long has the attorney been in practice in Georgia?

☞ What percentage of the attorney's cases involve divorce cases or other family law matters? (Don't expect an exact answer, but you should get a rough estimate that is at least twenty percent.)

☞ How long will it take? (Don't expect an exact answer, but the attorney should be able to give you an average range and discuss things which may make a difference).

If you get acceptable answers to these questions, it's time to ask yourself the following questions about the lawyer:

☞ Do you feel comfortable talking to the lawyer?

☞ Is the lawyer friendly toward you?

☞ Does the lawyer seem confident in himself or herself?

☞ Does the lawyer seem to be straight-forward with you, and able to explain things so you understand?

Some part of your evaluation may include the attorney's office. You should probably expect to see some evidence of computerization to help keep your costs down, but you will have your own opinions as to whether you prefer your professionals to be more or less technologically inclined. Also, the attorney's office and car may provide some clue to his success, but beware of relying on just the image. My grandfather told me that the solvency of any professional firm is inversely proportional to the expense of the office. In general, that has proven to be sound advice.

Your attorney should not act like he is too important for you, nor should you be looking for a "best friend." Domestic crises are times of tremendous emotional upheaval, and you are entitled to someone who will be absolutely straightforward, even if there is unpleasant information to convey.

Call the State Bar Association to see if there are any unresolved complaints against the attorney. Domestic relations cases are fairly high on the list of State Bar complaints, so don't be surprised if your attorney has been involved in an investigation. However, an inordinate number of unhappy clients is probably a bad omen.

Finally, how accessible is he or she? Is the attorney's residence number in the phone book or does he give clients his home phone number for emergencies? Does he wear a telephone pager or have a service for after-hours crises? Do not expect much sympathy from an attorney you try to call in the wee hours of the morning to have him referee a domestic argument, but it may be comforting to know that he or she can be reached in an emergency.

If you get satisfactory answers, you probably have a lawyer with whom you will be able to work. Most clients are happy with an attorney who makes them feel comfortable.

Working With a Lawyer

You will work best with your attorney if you keep an open, honest and friendly attitude. You should also consider the following suggestions.

Start early. Do your research before a crisis starts, while you have an opportunity to make decisions based on considered judgment rather than emergencies. Attorneys are trained to work in emergency situations, but the environment is expensive and the results more uncertain.

Leave your embarrassment at home. You will probably be discussing personal details with your attorney that you may never have mentioned to your best friend. Your sexual and social practices are going to be a topic of conversation…if this type of frank discussion is unpleasant, you better prepare for it.

Ask questions. If you want to know something or if you don't understand something, ask your attorney. If you don't understand the answer, tell your attorney and ask him or her to explain it again. There are many points of law that many lawyers don't fully understand, so you shouldn't be embarrassed to ask questions. Many people who say they had a bad experience with a lawyer either didn't ask enough questions, or had a lawyer who wouldn't take the time to explain things to them. If your lawyer isn't taking the time to explain what he's doing, it may be time to look for a new lawyer.

Give your lawyer complete information. Anything you tell your attorney is confidential. An attorney can lose his license to practice if he reveals information without your permission. So don't hold back, even if the issues are extremely personal. Tell your lawyer everything, even if it doesn't seem important to you. There are many things which seem unimportant to a non-attorney, but can change the outcome of a case. Also, don't hold something back because you are afraid it will hurt your case. It will definitely hurt your case if your lawyer doesn't find out about it until he hears it in court from your spouse's attorney! But if he knows in advance, he can plan to eliminate or reduce damage to your case.

Accept reality. Listen to what your lawyer tells you about the law and the system. It will do you no good to argue because the law or the system doesn't work the way you think it should. For example, if your lawyer tells you that the judge can't hear your case for two weeks, don't try demanding that he set an emergency hearing tomorrow. By refusing to accept reality, you are only setting yourself up for disappointment. And remember: It's not your attorney's fault that the system isn't perfect, or that the law doesn't say what you'd like it to say.

Be patient. This applies to being patient with the system (which is often slow as we discussed earlier), as well as with your attorney. Don't expect your lawyer to return your phone call within an hour. He may not be able to return it the same day either. Most lawyers are very busy, and over-worked. It is rare that a busy attorney can maintain a full case-load and still make each client feel as if he is the only client.

Talk to the secretary. Your lawyer's secretary can be a valuable source of information. So be friendly and get to know him. Often she will be able to answer your questions and you won't get a bill for the time you talk to him.

Let your attorney deal with your spouse. It is your lawyer's job to communicate with your spouse, or with your spouse's lawyer. Let him do his job. Many lawyers have had clients lose or damage their cases when the client decides to say or do something on their own. However, if lawyers are involved, and the parties wish to settle the case themselves but the lawyers seem to be part of the problem rather than part of the solution...remember that attorneys are ultimately employees who can be hired and fired.

Be on time. This applies to appointments with your lawyer, and especially to court hearings.

Keeping your case moving. Many lawyers operate on the old principle of the squeaking wheel gets the oil. Work on a case often gets put off until a deadline is near, an emergency develops, or the client calls. There is a reason for this. After many years of education (and the expense of that education), lawyers hope to earn the income due a professional. This is difficult with a great many attorneys competing for clients, and the high cost of office overhead. Many lawyers find it necessary to take more cases than can be effectively handled in order to make an acceptable living. That is why many attorneys work sixty-five hours a week or more. Your task is to become a squeaking wheel that doesn't squeak too much. Whenever you talk to your lawyer ask the following questions:

- ☛ What is the next step?

- ☛ When do you expect it to be done?

☞ When should I talk to you next?

If you don't hear from the lawyer when you expect, call him the following day. Don't remind him that he didn't call; just ask how things are going.

How to save money. Of course you don't want to spend unnecessary money for an attorney. Here are a few things you can do to avoid excess legal fees:

☞ Don't make unnecessary phone calls to your lawyer.

☞ Give information to the secretary whenever possible.

☞ Direct questions to the secretary. He'll refer to the attorney if he can't answer it.

☞ Plan your phone calls so you can get to the point, and take less of your attorney's time.

☞ If you leave a message on an answering machine, or voice mail, leave the number at which you can be reached. Often attorneys will return calls from court, pay phones, or car phones, and they do not have access to your personal phone numbers. Make it easy for them.

☞ Do some of the "leg work" yourself. Pick up and deliver papers yourself, for example. Ask your attorney what you can do to assist with your case.

☞ Be prepared for appointments. Have all related papers with you, plan your visit to get to the point, and make an outline of what you want to discuss and what questions you want to ask.

☞ ***Be smart!*** Think about the consequences of what you want to gain from a settlement. It is nuts to pay a lawyer $100 to fight for a lawnmower that you can buy used for $50. Similarly, a difference of $20 per week in child support for a two year old child amounts to $16,640.00 during the time the child is dependent on child support. It is probably worth it to spend a few bucks making sure this number is a low, or as high, as possible, but not worth arguing about the lawnmower.

Pay your attorney bill when it's due. No client gets prompt attention like a client who pays his or her lawyer on time. However, you are entitled to an itemized bill, showing what the attorney did and how much time it took. Many attorneys will have you sign an agreement that states how you will be charged, what is included in the hourly fee, and what is extra. Review your bill carefully. There are numerous stories of people paying an attorney $500 or $1,000 in advance, only to have the attorney make a few phone calls to the spouse's lawyer, then ask for more money. If your attorney asks for $500 or $1,000 in advance, you should be sure that you and the lawyer agree on what is to be done for this fee. For $500 you should at least expect to have a petition prepared, filed with the court, and served on your spouse (although the filing and service fees will probably be extra).

Firing your lawyer. If you find that you can no longer work with your lawyer, or don't trust your lawyer, it is time to either go it alone or get a new attorney. You will need to send your lawyer a letter stating that you no longer desire his services, and are discharging him from your case. Also state that you will be coming by his office the following week to pick up your file. (Of course, you will need to settle any remaining fees charged.) The attorney does not have to give you his own notes or other work he has in progress, but he must give you the essential contents of your file (such as copies of papers already filed or prepared and billed for, and any documents you provided). If he refuses to give you this information, the state bar association may be contacted regarding a grievance procedure. Quite frankly, most attorneys would much rather work out their problems with you than defend themselves from a complaint to the bar association.

EVALUATING YOUR SITUATION 4

The following things should be done or considered before you begin the divorce process.

YOUR SPOUSE

First, you need to evaluate your situation with respect to your spouse. Have you both already agreed to get a divorce? If not, what kind of reaction do you expect from him or her? Your expected reaction can determine how you will proceed. If he or she reacts in a rational manner, you can probably use the uncontested procedure. But if you expect an extremely emotional, and possibly violent reaction, you will need to take steps to protect yourself, your children, and your property; and will have to start out expecting to use the contested procedure.

You were warned on the back cover of this book not to let your spouse find this book, and it was for a very good reason. Unless you and your spouse have already decided together to get a divorce, you don't want your spouse to know you are thinking about filing for divorce. This is a defense tactic, although it may not seem that way at first. If your spouse thinks you are planning a divorce, he or she may do things to prevent you from getting a fair result. These things include withdrawing money from bank accounts, hiding information about income, and hiding assets. So don't let on until you've collected all of the information you will need and are about to file with the court, or until you are prepared to protect yourself from violence, if necessary.

Caution: Tactics such as withdrawing money from bank accounts and hiding assets are dangerous. If you try any of these things you risk looking like the "bad guy" before the judge. This can result in anything from having disputed matters resolved in your spouse's favor, to being ordered to produce the assets (or be jailed for contempt of court). Georgia also requires that the assets of the parties in a divorce be held in "trust" until the ownership is resolved. It is a dangerous situation to take items that belong to both of you and try and dispose of them yourself.

Theoretically, the "system" would prefer you to keep evidence of the assets (such as photographs, sales receipts, or bank statements), to present to the judge if your spouse hides them. Then your spouse will be the bad guy and risk being jailed. However, once your spouse has taken assets, and hidden them, or sold them and spent the money, even a contempt order may not get the money or assets back. If you determine that you need to get the assets in order to keep your spouse from hiding or disposing of them, be sure you keep them in a safe place, and disclose them on your FINANCIAL AFFIDAVIT (Form 13). Do not dispose of them. If your spouse claims you took them, you can explain to the judge why you were afraid that your spouse would dispose of them and that you merely got them out of his or her reach.

GATHERING INFORMATION

It is extremely important that you collect all of the financial information you can get. This information should include originals or copies of the following:

☞ Your most recent income tax return (and your spouse's if you filed separately).

☞ The most recent W-2 tax forms for yourself and your spouse.

☞ Any other income reporting papers (such as interest, stock dividends, etc.).

☞ Your spouse's most recent paystub, hopefully showing year-to-date earnings (otherwise try to get copies of all paystubs since the beginning of the year).

☞ Deeds to all real estate; and titles to cars, boats, or other vehicles.

☞ Your and your spouse's will.

☞ Life insurance policies.

☞ Stocks, bonds or other investment papers.

☞ Pension or retirement fund papers and statements.

☞ Health insurance card and papers.

☞ Bank account or credit union statements.

☞ Your spouse's social security number, and driver's license number.

☞ Names, addresses, and phone numbers of your spouse's employer, close friends, and family members.

☞ Credit card statements, mortgage documents, and other credit and debt papers.

☞ A list of vehicles, furniture, appliances, tools, etc., owned by you and your spouse. (See the next section in this chapter on "Property and Debts" for forms and a detailed discussion of what to include.)

☞ Copies of bills or receipts for recurring, regular expenses, such as electric, gas or other utilities, car insurance, etc.

☞ Copies of bills, receipts, insurance forms, or medical records for any unusual medical expenses (including for recurring or continuous medical conditions) for yourself, your spouse, or your children.

☞ Any other papers showing what you and your spouse earn, own, or owe.

☞ Any information about personal injury or workers compensation cases your spouse may be involved with, as well as any inheritance, trust, or estate issues with which he or she may be involved.

Make copies of as many of these papers as possible, and keep them in a safe and private place (where your spouse won't find them). Try to make copies of new papers as they come in, especially as you get close to filing court papers, and as you get close to a court hearing. Once a client came into my office with copies of papers carelessly left in her husband's briefcase...it was the financial reports from a second set of accounts that he was using at his business and of which she was completely unaware. That case settled very promptly when her husband's attorney was presented with our information. My client had no idea what she had copied.

PROPERTY AND DEBTS

This section is designed to help you get a rough idea of where things stand regarding the division of your property and debts, and to prepare you for completing the court papers you will need to file. The following sections will deal with the questions of alimony, child support, custody and visitation. If you are still not sure whether you want a divorce, these sections may help you to decide.

PROPERTY   Trying to determine how to divide assets and debts can be difficult. Under Georgia's *equitable distribution* law, assets and debts are separated into two categories: *marital* (meaning it is both yours and your spouse's), and *nonmarital* (meaning it is yours or your spouse's alone). In making this distinction the following rules apply:

1. If the asset or debt was acquired after the date you were married, it is presumed to be a marital asset of debt. It is up to you or your spouse to prove otherwise.

2. In order to be a nonmarital asset or debt, it must have been acquired before the date of your marriage. Also, it is nonmarital if you acquired it through a gift or inheritance (as long as it wasn't a gift from your spouse), and this includes income from nonmarital property. (Example 1: Rent you receive from an investment property you had before you got married.) If you exchange one of these assets of debts after your marriage, it may still be nonmarital. (Example 2: You had a $6,000 car before you got married. After the marriage, you traded it for a different $6,000 car. The new car is probably also nonmarital.) Finally, you and your spouse may sign a written agreement that certain assets and debts are to be considered nonmarital, these agreements, if executed prior to the marriage, may be enforceable, and may not. Unfortunately, Georgia law does not favor contracts in contemplation of marriage (sometimes called *prenuptial agreements*), and they can be looked at very closely. Most court arguments over property involve controversies over what is marital property and what is not. If this becomes a contested issue in your case, and valuable property is at stake, you may want to consult a lawyer.

3. Marital assets and debts are those which were acquired during your marriage, even if they were acquired by you or your spouse individually. This also includes the increase in value of a nonmarital asset during the marriage, or due to the use of marital funds to pay for or improve the property. Usually, all rights accrued during the marriage in pension, retirement, profit-sharing, insurance, and similar plans are marital assets. It is also

possible for one spouse to make a gift of nonmarital property to the other spouse, thereby making it marital property.

4. Real estate that is in both names is considered marital property, and it's up to the spouse claiming otherwise to prove it.

5. Finally, the value of an asset, as well as the question of whether an asset or debt is marital or nonmarital, are determined as of the date of the settlement agreement, or the date the petition was filed, whichever is first. However, Georgia law says that, even if you separate, marital assets can still accumulate. (This is another reason to watch out for separate maintenance.)

The following information will assist you in completing the PROPERTY INVENTORY (Form 1 in appendix C of this book). This form is a list of all of your property, and key information about that property. You will notice that this form is divided into nine columns, designated as follows:

☞   Column (1): You will check the box in this column if that piece of property is nonmarital property. This is property that either you or your spouse acquired before you were married, or which were given to you or your spouse separately, or which were inherited by you or your spouse separately.

☞   Column (2): Describe the property in this column. A discussion regarding what information should go in this column will follow.

☞   Column (3): This column is used to write in the serial number, account number, or other number which will help clearly identify that piece of property.

☞   Column (4): This is for the current market value of the property.

☞   Column (5): This will show how much money is owed on the property, if any.

☞   Column (6): Subtract the Balance Owed from the Value. This will show how much the property is worth to you (your *equity*).

☛ Column (7): This column will show the current legal owner of the property. (H) designates the husband, (W) the wife, and (J) is for jointly owned property (in both of your names).

☛ Column (8): This column will be checked for those pieces of property you expect the husband will keep.

☛ Column (9): This column is for the property you expect the wife will keep.

Use columns (1) through (7) to list your property, including the following:

Cash. List the name of the bank, credit union, etc., and the account number, for each account. This includes savings and checking accounts, and certificates of deposit (CDs). The balance of each account should be listed in the columns entitled VALUE and EQUITY. (Leave the BALANCE OWED column blank.) Make copies of the most recent bank statements for each account.

Stocks and bonds. All stocks, bonds or other "paper investments" should be listed. Write down the number of shares and the name of the company or other organization that issued them. Also copy any notation such as "common" or "preferred" stock or shares. This information can be obtained from the stock certificate itself, or from a statement from the stock broker. Make a copy of the certificate or the statement.

Real estate. List each piece of property you and your spouse own. The description might include a street address for the property, a subdivision name and lot number, or anything that lets you know what piece of property you are referring to. There probably won't be an ID number, although you might use the county's tax number. Real estate (or any other property) may be in both of your names (joint), in your spouse's name alone, or in your name alone. The only way to know for sure is to look at the deed to the property. (If you can't find a copy of the deed, try to find mortgage papers or payment coupons, homeowners insurance papers, or a property tax assessment notice.) The owners of property are usually referred to on the deed as the *grantees*. In assigning a value to the property, consider the market value, which is how much you could probably sell the property for. This might be what similar houses in your neighborhood have sold for recently. You might also consider how much you paid for the property, or how much the property is insured for. *Do not* use the tax assessment value, as this is usually considerably lower than the market value.

Vehicles. This category includes cars, trucks, motor homes, recreational vehicles (RVs), motorcycles, boats, trailers, airplanes, and any other means of transportation for which the State requires a title and registration. Your description should include the following information (which can usually be found on the title or on the vehicle itself):

- ☞ Year it was made.

- ☞ Make: The name of the manufacturer, such as "Ford," "Honda," "Chris Craft," etc.

- ☞ Model: You know it's a Ford, but is it a Mustang, an LTD, or an Aerostar: The model may be a name, a number, a series of letters, or a combination of these.

- ☞ Serial Number: This is most likely found on the vehicle, as well as on the title or registration. This information is required to keep you from owing the State of Georgia a transfer tax of 10% of the value of the vehicle as a result of changing the name on the title.

Make a copy of the title or registration. Regarding a value, you can go to the public library and ask to look at the *blue book* for cars, trucks, or whatever it is you're looking for. A blue book (which may actually be yellow, black or any other color) gives the average values for used vehicles. Your librarian can help you find what you need. Another source is to look in the classified advertising section of a newspaper to see what similar vehicles are selling for. You might also try calling a dealer to see if he can give you a rough idea of the value. Be sure you take into consideration the condition of the vehicle.

Furniture. List all furniture as specifically as possible. You should include the type of piece (such as sofa, coffee table, etc.), the color, and if you know it, the manufacturer, line name, or the style. Furniture usually won't have a serial number, although if you find one be sure to write it on the list. Just estimate a value, unless you just know what it's worth.

Appliances, electronic equipment, yard machines, etc. This category includes such things as refrigerators, lawn mowers, and power tools. Again, estimate a value, unless you are familiar enough with them to simply know what they are worth. There are too many different makes, models, accessories and age factors to be able to figure out a value otherwise. These items will probably have a make, model, and serial number on them. You may have to look on the back, bottom, or other hidden place for the serial number, but try to find it.

Jewelry and other valuables. You don't need to list inexpensive, or costume jewelry. And you can plan on keeping your own personal watches, rings, etc. However, if you own an expensive piece, then you should include it in your list along with an estimated value. Be sure to include silverware, original art, gold, coin collections, etc. Again, be as detailed and specific as possible.

Life insurance with cash surrender value. This is any life insurance policy which you may cash in or borrow against, and therefore has value. If you cannot find a cash surrender value in the papers you have, you can call the insurance company and ask.

Other "big ticket" items. This is simply a general reference to anything of significant value that doesn't fit in one of the categories already discussed. Examples might be a portable spa, an above-ground swimming pool, golf clubs, guns, pool tables, camping or fishing equipment, or farm animals or machinery.

Pensions and military benefits. The division of pensions, and military and retirement benefits, can be a complicated matter. Whenever these types of benefits are involved, you will need to consult an attorney or a CPA to determine the value of the benefits and how they should be divided. Be sure to read the section in chapter 11 on pension plans.

What not to list. You will not need to list your clothing and other personal effects. Pots, pans, dishes, and cooking utensils ordinarily do not need to be listed, unless they have some unusually high value.

Once you have completed your list, go back through it and try to determine who should end up with each item. The ideal situation is for both you and your spouse to go through the list together, and divide the items fairly. However, if this is not possible, you will need to offer a reasonable settlement to the judge. Consider each item, and make a checkmark in either column (8) or (9) to designate whether that item should go to the husband or wife. You may make the following assumptions:

1. Your nonmarital property will go to you.

2. Your spouse's nonmarital property will go to your spouse.

3. You should get the items that only you use.

4. Your spouse should get the items only used by your spouse.

5. The remaining items should be divided, evening out the total value of all the marital property, and taking into consideration who would really want that item. The general rule is that each party is entitled to a property division of one-half of the assets, and one-half of the liabilities of the marriage.

To somewhat equally divide your property (we're only talking about marital property here), you first need to know the total value of your property. First of all, do not count the value of the nonmarital items. Add the remaining amounts in the EQUITY column of Form 1, which will give you an approximate value of all marital property.

In an uncontested case, often the parties simply go room by room, with each party taking turns picking items that they particularly wish to keep. This arrangement works best when the parties can keep in mind that they were at one time friends and lovers, and that the current circumstances should be kept as pleasant as possible.

If it comes time for the hearing and you and your spouse are still arguing over some or all of the items on your list, you'll be glad that you made copies of the documents relating to the property on your list. Arguments over the value of property may need to be resolved by hiring appraisers to set a value; however, you'll have to pay the appraiser a fee. Dividing your property will be discussed further in later chapters. (See chapter 8 for information on dividing property in contested cases).

DEBTS

This section relates to the DEBT INVENTORY (Form 2), which will list your debts. Although there are cases where, for example, the wife gets a car but the husband makes the payments, generally whoever gets the property also gets the debt owed on that property. This seems to be a fair arrangement in most cases. On Form 2 you will list each debt owed by you or your spouse. As with nonmarital property, there is also nonmarital debt. This is any debt incurred before you were married, that is yours alone. Form 2 contains a column for "N-M" debts, which should be checked for each nonmarital debt. You will be responsible for your nonmarital debts, and your spouse will be responsible for his or hers.

To complete the DEBT INVENTORY (Form 2), list each debt as follows:

- Column (1): Check if this is a nonmarital debt.

- Column (2): Write in the name and address of the creditor (the bank, company, or person the debt is owed to).

- Column (3): Write in the account, loan, or mortgage number.

- Column (4): Write in any notes to help identify what the loan was for (such as "Christmas gifts," "Vacation," etc.).

- Column (5): Write in the amount of the monthly payment.

☞ Column (6): Write in the balance still owed on the loan.

☞ Column (7): Write in the date (approximately) when the loan was made.

☞ Column (8): Note whether the account is in the husband's name (H), the wife's name (W), or jointly in both names (J).

☞ Columns (9) & (10): These columns note who will be responsible for the debt after the divorce. As with your property, each of you will keep your non-marital debts, and the remainder should be divided taking into consideration who will keep the property the loan was for and equally dividing the debt. (See chapter 7 for information on dividing debts in contested cases).

CHILD CUSTODY AND VISITATION

As with everything else in divorce, things are ideal when both parties can agree on the question of custody of the children. Generally the judge will accept any agreement you reach, provided it doesn't appear that your agreement will cause harm to your children.

With respect to child custody, the Georgia law makes three significant statements. First, the Court is to inquire as to the best interests of the child and that the preferred method of custody is to maximize the child's contact with both parents. Second, the statutes state very clearly that the party not in default is entitled to custody. How each judge resolves this conflict is the subject of much discussion among attorneys and parents, but a judge's decision, if carefully made, is rarely if ever overturned. Third, if the child is over the age of fourteen, he or she may choose with which parent to live.

Although there is no law supporting it, you may expect that most judges are from the old school of thought on the subject of custody and believe that (all things being equal) a young child is better off with the mother. The judge may go to great lengths to justify an award of custody to the mother. It happens day after day throughout the state, and it's a reality you may have to deal with. If you are the husband, and believe your particular circumstances are such that you would be a better choice as the parent, be prepared to determine how much "justice" you can afford.

Joint custody is a great idea in its concept, but it is usually not a very practical one. Originally, this type of custody contemplated parents separated by great distances who each kept the child for an extended period of time. The term has evolved to mean a significant shared custody arrangement with quality time divided more or less along equal bounds. When it works, it works wonderfully. When it does not work, there are some predictable problems. Very few parents can put aside their anger toward each other to agree on what is best for their child.

Joint custody often even makes this worse and leads to more fighting. And even if joint custody is ordered, a child can only have one primary residence. So the judge may still decide which parent the child will mainly live with, as well as how decisions regarding such things as education, and medical and dental care will be made.

If you and your spouse cannot agree on how these matters will be handled, you will be leaving this important decision up to the judge. The judge cannot possibly know your child as well as you and your spouse, so doesn't it make sense for you to work this out yourselves? Otherwise you are leaving the decision to a stranger.

If the judge must decide the issue, there is only one question to be answered: "What is in the best interest of the child?" The judge could consider such things as:

- ☛ Which parent is most likely to allow the other to visit with the child.

- ☛ The love, affection, and other emotional ties existing between the child and each parent.

☛ The ability and willingness of each parent to provide the child with food, clothing, medical care, and other material needs.

☛ The length of time the child has lived with either parent in a stable environment.

☛ The permanence, as a family unit, of the proposed custodial home. (This relates to where one of the parties will be getting remarried immediately after the divorce, or, more often, to petitions to change custody at a later date.)

☛ The moral fitness of each parent.

☛ The mental and physical health of each parent.

☛ The home, school, and community record of the child.

☛ The preference of the child, providing the child is of sufficient intelligence and understanding.

☛ Any other fact the judge decides is relevant.

I have had one superior court judge tell me that he uses the *diaper rule* in the case of arguments involving small children. For the decision as to the custodial parent, that judge wants to know who has changed the bulk of the diapers, prepared the bulk of the meals, taken the child to the doctor, and read the child to sleep at night. While all judges certainly are not following this formula, you might keep it in mind…I have.

It is impossible to predict the outcome of a custody battle, and anyone who tells you otherwise is nuts. There are too many factors and individual circumstances to make such a guess. The only exception is where one parent is clearly unfit and the other can prove it, and unfitness can be awfully subjective.

Drug abuse is probably the most common charge against a spouse, but unless there has been an arrest and conviction it is difficult to prove to a judge. In general, don't charge your spouse with being unfit unless you can prove it.

Child abuse is also a common charge, but this explosive issue should not be raised lightly. Judges are not impressed with unfounded allegations, and they can do more harm than good.

Under some recent Georgia court decisions, homosexuality, by itself, cannot be a factor in a custody decision.

If your children are older (not infants), it may be a good idea to seriously consider their preference for with whom they would like to live. Your "fairness" and respect for their wishes may benefit you in the long run. Just be sure that you keep in close contact with them and visit them often.

Georgia also allows children over the age of fourteen to elect their custodial parent. A form is included in appendix C. The child can change their mind at trial, and the judge does not have to agree with the child, but most of the time, the minor's election carries a tremendous amount of weight.

CHILD SUPPORT

Judges in Georgia are generally constrained to follow the Uniform Superior Court Guidelines for Child Support, and a copy of these guidelines is included as Schedule A in Form 3. The judge will probably not go along with any agreement you and your spouse reach if your agreement does not conform to these guidelines, and he will take special interest in knowing that the child's needs are being met.

HOW CHILD SUPPORT IS DETERMINED

The following information and the CHILD SUPPORT GUIDELINES WORKSHEET (Form 3), will help you get an idea of the proper amount of child support for your situation. Here you are only using Form 3 to try to get a rough idea of the amount of child support to expect. Later, when you might have more precise income information about your spouse, you will review this for a more accurate figure.

The information on Form 3 will also help you to fill out part of the DOMESTIC RELATIONS FINANCIAL AFFIDAVIT (Form 12), if you need to complete that form. Where an agreement cannot be reached the following procedure will be used:

To keep from having to make special findings justifying an unconventional decision, you can count on the court using the percentages listed below. The "Percentage of Gross Income" gives the possible range the judge may use, and the "Usual Percentage Applied" gives the percentage that is most typically used:

Number of Children	Percentage of Gross Income	Usual Percentage Applied
1	17-23 percent	20 percent
2	23-28 percent	25 percent
3	25-32 percent	30 percent
4	29-35 percent	33 percent
5 (or more)	31-37 percent	35 percent

To justify an award outside of these guidelines, special circumstances must be shown, including:

1. Ages of the children.

2. A child's medical costs or extraordinary needs.

3. Education costs.

4. Day care costs.

5. Shared physical custody arrangements that may include extended visitation.

6. A party's obligations to another household.

7. Income that a spouse could make if they wanted to work.

8. Benefits that a spouse is getting which are not included in their salary.

9. Additional support, such as payment of a mortgage.

10. A spouse's own extraordinary needs, such as significant medical expenses.

11. Extreme economic conditions, such as high income (usually over $75,000 gross a year, or very high debt loads).

12. An historical pattern of spending on the children that puts the parties out of the general range of support, such as always sending the children to expensive camps or private schools that were not really within the parties means.

13. In-kind contributions of the parties.

14. The income of the custodial parent.

15. Economic factors within the community.

GROSS INCOME   The first thing you will need to do is determine your *gross income*. This is basically your income before any deductions for taxes, social security, etc. The following money sources are considered part of gross income:

- ☞ Salary or wages.

- ☞ Overtime, commissions, bonuses, allowances, tips, etc.

- ☞ Business income from self-employment, partnerships, corporations, and independent contracts (gross receipts, minus ordinary and necessary expenses).

- ☞ Disability benefits.

- ☞ Worker's compensation.

- ☞ Unemployment compensation.

- ☞ Pension, retirement, or annuity payments.

☛ Social security benefits.

☛ Alimony received from a previous marriage.

☛ Interest and dividends.

☛ Rental Income (gross receipts, minus ordinary and necessary expenses—but not depreciation).

☛ Income from royalties, trusts, or estates.

☛ Reimbursed expenses to the extent they reduce living expenses (such as a rent allowance, or the value of an apartment provided by your employer).

☛ Gains derived from dealings in property, unless the gain is non-recurring.

These categories should all be included in your calculation of gross monthly income on Form 3. If you are trying to determine your potential liability, use your income. If you are trying to decide how much your spouse should pay, use his or her income. Then write in the total gross income on line 1 of Form 3, which is on the first page of the form. If you voluntarily reduce your income, or quit your job, the judge can refuse to recognize the reduction or loss of income. This is *imputed income*. The only exception is where you are required to take such an action to stay home and care for your child. If this question comes up, the judge will decide whether you need to stay home, so be ready to explain your reasons. If you have any imputed income, fill in the amount on line 2. Total lines 1 and 2, and fill in the total on line 3.

CALCULATING
CHILD SUPPORT

Once you determine the payor's ("paying spouse" in Form 3) gross monthly income, turn back to the child support guidelines table in Schedule A of Form 3. Find the number of children support will be paid for, then read across to get the high and low percentage. Multiply the monthly gross income (from line 3) by the high percentage figure, and fill in the answer on line 4 under the word "HIGH." Then multiply the monthly gross income by the low percentage figure, and fill in the answer on line 4 under the word "LOW." This will give you the monthly range of child support you can expect.

Now, take the figures from line 4, multiply each one by 12, then divide by 52. This will give you the range of the weekly support obligation.

Example: The payor's gross monthly income is $2,000 and there are two children. According to Schedule A in Form 3, the support obligation for two children is between 23% and 28%. Therefore, the monthly support obligation would be between $460.00 ($2,000 x .23) and $560.00 ($2,000 x .28). The weekly support obligation would be between $106.15 ($460 x 12, divided by 52), and $129.23 ($560 x 12, divided by 52).

ALIMONY

Georgia law provides that alimony may be granted to either the husband or the wife. (See appendix B, for the statute explaining the factors involved in deciding the issue of alimony.) In reality there are few cases in which a wife will be ordered to pay alimony to her husband.

TYPES OF ALIMONY

There are two types of alimony:

1. *Temporary alimony.* This is for a limited period of time, and is to enable one of the spouses to get the education or training necessary to find a job. This is usually awarded where one of the parties has not been working during the marriage.

2. *Permanent alimony.* This continues for a long period of time, possibly until the death or remarriage of the party receiving the alimony. This is typically awarded where one of the parties is unable to work due to age, or a physical or mental illness, or for reasons of fairness.

ALIMONY FACTORS

The only common area in which alimony is excluded is where the spouse seeking alimony is guilty of adultery, uncondoned by the other innocent party, and the adultery is the cause of the divorce. However, the factors considered in determining the type and amount of alimony also give clues as to when alimony might be awarded.

The law requires the judge to consider the following factors:

1. The standard of living established during the marriage.

2. The length of time the parties were married.

3. The age and the physical and emotional condition of each party.

4. The financial resources of each party.

5. The time necessary for either party to obtain education and training in order to obtain appropriate employment.

6. The contribution of each party to the marriage (such as services rendered in homemaking, child care, and the education and career building of the other party).

7. The condition of the parties, including their separate estate, earning capacity, and fixed liabilities.

8. Any other relevant economic factor.

9. Any other factor the judge finds necessary to reach a fair result. As an alternative to alimony, you may want to try to negotiate to receive a greater percentage of the property instead. This may be less of a hassle in the long run, but it may change the tax consequences of your divorce. (See chapter 12 regarding taxes.) Be prepared, though, to justify any distribution that changes your personal tax situation. The IRS can be rather particular about schemes designed to evade taxes.

WHICH PROCEDURE TO USE

Technically, there are two divorce procedures. These are:

1. Uncontested Divorce Procedure

2. Contested Divorce Procedure

The uncontested and contested use some of the same forms, but the contested will require additional steps.

Chapter 6 describes the uncontested procedure, and chapter 7 describes the contested divorce. You should read this entire book once before you begin filling out any court forms.

> *Caution:* Before you can use any procedure you or your spouse must have lived in Georgia for at least six months before filing your petition.

UNCONTESTED DIVORCE PROCEDURE
The uncontested procedure is designed for those who are in agreement (or can reach an agreement) about how to divide the property, custody, the amounts of support, and visitation. This is also referred to as a *consent* divorce. The uncontested procedure may also be used when your spouse does not respond to your petition. If your spouse cannot be located you can use the same forms, but although you can get a divorce and custody, it is sometimes difficult to get any alimony, to get property your spouse currently has, or to make your disappeared spouse responsible for any debts.

CONTESTED DIVORCE PROCEDURE
The contested procedure will be necessary where you and your spouse are arguing over any single issue, or combination of issues, and can't resolve it. This may be the result of disagreement over custody of the children, the payment of child support or alimony, the division of your property, or any combination of these items. The section of this book dealing with the contested procedure builds on the uncontested procedure section. So, first you will need to read chapter 6 to get a basic understanding of the forms and procedures, then read chapter 7 for

additional instructions on handling the contested situation. Be sure to read through both chapters before you start filling out any forms. Keep in mind that a contested divorce may increase the likelihood that you will find the services of a lawyer to be valuable, either to consult or to totally handle your case.

General Procedures and Forms 5

An Introduction to Legal Forms

Most of the forms in this book follow forms approved by statute and tested by practice. As this book is being printed, "official" forms have not yet been released for distribution by the Bar Association. The forms in this book are legally correct, however, one occasionally encounters a troublesome clerk or judge who is very particular about how he or she wants the forms.

When you go to file your forms, don't be surprised if you get "interrogated" by the clerk. Some courts object to a fill-in-the-blank format, which will require you to re-type the entire form with the appropriate information included. Although there is no good reason for this requirement, re-typing the forms to satisfy the clerk will be easier, cheaper, and less time-consuming than hiring a lawyer to sue the clerk (and possibly the judge) to try to force acceptance of the pre-printed forms.

If you encounter any problem with the forms in this book being accepted by the clerk or the judge, you can try one or more of the following:

- ☛ Ask the clerk or judge what is wrong with your form, then try to change it to suit the clerk or judge.

- Ask the clerk or judge if any Bar Association forms are available yet. If they are, find out where you can get them, get them and use them. The instructions in this book will still help you to fill them out.

- Consult a lawyer.

To use the forms in appendix C, you will need to photocopy the forms in this book, because the forms you file with the clerk should only have writing on one side. This will also allow you to have the blank forms in case you make a mistake. The instructions in this book will tell you to "type in" certain information, and believe it or not, typed information is required under the Uniform Rules of The Superior Court. While some clerks will allow handwritten forms, it is best not to take the chance. In an emergency, just be sure your handwriting can be easily read, or the clerk may not accept your papers for filing regardless of his or her sympathy for your situation.

Each form is referred to by both the title of the form and a form number. Be sure to check the form number because some of the forms have similar titles. The form number is found in the top outside corner of the first page of each form. Also, a list of the forms, by both number and name, is found at the beginning of appendix C.

You will notice that most of the forms in appendix C of this book have the same heading. For the most part, this is a clue. Generally, the forms without this heading are not filed with the court, but are for your use only. However, the top portion of each of these court forms will all be completed in the same manner. The heading at the very top of the form tells which court your case is filed in. You will need to type in the name of the appropriate county where the court is located.

Next, you need to type your full name, and your spouse's, on the lines at the left side of the form, above the words "Plaintiff" and "Defendant" respectively. Do not use nicknames or shortened versions of names. You should use the names as they appear on your marriage license, if possible. You won't be able to type in a "Case Number" until after you file your PETITION FOR DIVORCE with the clerk. The clerk will assign a case number and will write it on your petition and any other papers you file with it. You must type in the case number on all papers you file later.

The top part of the form is called the *style* of the case, and when completed, the top portion of your forms should look something like the following example:

IN THE SUPERIOR COURT OF THE COUNTY OF _____FULTON_____

STATE OF GEORGIA

RHETT BUTLER   *

          Plaintiff   *

                                               *   Civil Action File Number

                                               *

     vs.   *

                                               *   _____

SCARLETT O'HARA BUTLER   *

          Defendant   *

FILING WITH THE COURT CLERK

DETERMINING WHICH COUNTY

Georgia has over 100 counties. Each county has a Superior Court, and each Superior Court has a clerk. As a general rule, if you and your spouse live in the same county, file with your county clerk. In most cases where you have separated, you must file your contested or uncontested divorce *in the county where your spouse lives*, if different from your own. If your spouse has only recently separated, and is temporarily residing in another county, while you have been in the same county for some time, you may want to file in your county and have the sheriff of the spouse's county serve your spouse. If this sounds somewhat complicated, it is. Hundreds of cases every year involve the question of which Georgia county is the proper county in which to bring suit. If your circumstances are complex, this is the type of question an attorney should be able to address at a modest fee.

Once you have decided which forms you need, and have them all prepared, it is time to file your case with the court clerk. First, make at least three copies of each form (the original for the clerk, one copy for yourself, one for your spouse, and one extra just in case the clerk asks for two copies or you decide to hire an attorney later).

Filing is actually about as simple as making a bank deposit, although the following information will help things go smoothly. Call the court clerk's office. You can find the phone number under the county government section of your phone directory. Ask the clerk the following questions (along with any other questions that come to mind, such as where the clerk's office is located and what their hours are):

☛ How much is the filing fee for a divorce?

☛ Does the court have any special forms that need to be filed with the petition? (If there are special forms that do not appear in this book, you will need to go down to the clerk's office and pick them up. There may be a fee, so ask.)

☛ How many copies of the petition and other forms do you need to file with the clerk?

Next, take your petition, and any other forms you determine you need, to the clerk's office. The clerk handles many different types of cases, so be sure to look for signs telling you which office or window to go to. You should be looking for signs that say such things as "Civil Division," "Superior Court Filing," etc. If it's too confusing, ask someone where you file a petition for divorce.

Once you've found the right place, simply hand the papers to the clerk and say, "I'd like to file this." The clerk will examine the papers, then do one of two things: either accept it for filing (and either collect the filing fee or direct you to where to pay it), or tell you that something is not correct. If you are told something is wrong, ask the clerk to explain to you what is wrong and how to correct the problem. Although clerks are not permitted to give legal advice, the types of problems they spot are usually very minor things that they can tell you how to correct. Often it is possible to figure out how to correct it from the way they explain what is wrong. Some clerks, due to busy schedules, or the fact that most clerks are not attorneys, try to avoid giving any specific advice. If the clerk will not take your papers, and will not tell you what the problem is, you might ask for the legal aid office, or perhaps ask an attorney to simply review your papers for a modest fee.

NOTIFYING YOUR SPOUSE

You don't need to worry about this section if you and your spouse are in total agreement about every aspect of the divorce. You both simply sign and file an AGREEMENT (Form 14). However, in all other cases, you are required to notify your spouse that you have filed for divorce. This gives your spouse a chance to respond to your PETITION FOR DIVORCE. If you are unable to find your spouse, you will also need to read chapter 11.

ACKNOWLEDGMENT OF SERVICE AND CONSENT TO JURISDICTION

If you and your spouse have agreed to all terms, it is customary to simply sign an ACKNOWLEDGMENT OF SERVICE AND CONSENT TO JURISDICTION (Form 23), which includes a paragraph in which the other party consents to the jurisdiction of the court, to be filed along with the PETITION FOR DIVORCE. This form is very simple. Put the name of the county in the first blank at the top of the form. Then write your name as "Plaintiff" and your spouse's name as "Defendant," both in the heading and twice in the body of the form. The clerk will give you the civil action file number when you sign this form. Have your spouse sign before a notary public on the line above the word "Defendant." If your spouse will not sign this form, go to the section below entitled "Sheriff's Entry of Service."

Along with the previous forms, at least one copy of the SUMMONS (Form 4) will be required. The information on the SUMMONS is identical to the information for either the ACKNOWLEDGMENT OF SERVICE AND CONSENT TO JURISDICTION (Form 23) or the SHERIFF'S ENTRY OF SERVICE (Form 5).

SUMMONS

To complete the SUMMONS (Form 4) you need to:

1. Complete the top portion according to the instructions at the beginning of this chapter, except type in your name and address on the lines above the word "PLAINTIFF," and your spouse's name and address on the lines above the word "DEFENDANT."

2. Type your name and address again in the space after the first paragraph. After your name type in the words "Pro Se." This form is designed for an attorney's name to go in this space, and "Pro Se" means that you do not have an attorney.

3. Go to the clerk's office, and have the clerk sign and date the Summons when you file your pleadings. The bottom portion of this form is for the sheriff deputy to complete when he serves your spouse.

SHERIFF'S ENTRY OF SERVICE

If your spouse will not sign an ACKNOWLEDGMENT OF SERVICE AND CONSENT TO JURISDICTION (Form 23), or for some reason simply can not, then use the SHERIFF'S ENTRY OF SERVICE (Form 5). A sheriff's deputy will personally deliver the papers to your spouse. Of course, you must give the sheriff accurate information about where your spouse can be found. If there are several addresses where your spouse might be found (such as home, a relative's, and work), enclose a letter to the sheriff with all of the addresses and any other information that may help the sheriff find your spouse (such as the hours your spouse works). The SHERIFF'S ENTRY OF SERVICE is the form the deputy will fill out and file with the clerk to verify that the papers were delivered (including the date and time they were delivered). The SHERIFF'S ENTRY OF SERVICE form in appendix C is an example of a commonly used form, but first call the Court Clerk in your county and ask if your county uses a particular form.

If you need to provide the sheriff with this form, use the SHERIFF'S ENTRY OF SERVICE (Form 5), and complete it as follows:

1. Type in the county and case number at the very top of the form.

2. In the upper right part of the form, type in your name on the line above the word "Plaintiff," and your spouse's name on the line above the word "Defendant." Place an "x" in the box after the word "Defendant." Type in your spouse's address on the line above the word "Address." Ignore the lines for a garnishee.

3. Type in your name and address on the lines below the words "Attorney or Plaintiff's Name & Address." Again, add the words "Pro Se" after your name.

4. Give this form to the sheriff, who will complete the rest of the form and file it with the court clerk after your spouse has been served. You may be able to pay the service fee (about $30.00) and leave the form with the court clerk when you file your Petition. The sheriff may also send you a copy, but you may need to check your file at the clerk's office to see if your spouse has been served. Since you are filing this action in the county of your spouse's residence, the clerk will probably accept the service fee when you file your petition. If not, call the county sheriff's office in the county where your spouse lives, and ask how much it will cost to have him or her served with divorce papers.

OTHER NOTICES   If a hearing on your case should be necessary, the notice of the hearing date and time is called a RULE NISI (Form 6). To complete Form 6:

1. Fill in the top portion of the form according to the instructions at the beginning of this chapter.

2. In the main paragraph, cross out either the word "Plaintiff" or the word "Defendant," whichever is appropriate. If you are the plaintiff, you would cross out the word "Defendant" in the first line; the word "Plaintiff" in the fourth line; and the word "Defendant" in the fifth line.

75

3. Fill in the date and time of the hearing, if you know it. Otherwise the clerk or judge's secretary can provide you with this information when you arrange a date and time.

4. Type your name on the line above the words "Pro Se," and your address and telephone number where indicated.

Take the RULE NISI form to the Clerk, who will assign a hearing date and time. If you have an ACKNOWLEDGMENT OF SERVICE AND CONSENT TO JURISDICTION, or if the Sheriff has already served the papers and your spouse has filed an Answer, just mail a copy of the RULE NISI to your spouse, along with a completed CERTIFICATE OF SERVICE (Form 7). If you have not filed an ACKNOWLEDGMENT OF SERVICE AND CONSENT TO JURISDICTION, and your spouse has not answered your PETITION FOR DIVORCE, the RULE NISI will have to be served by the sheriff in the same manner as described above in the section on "Sheriff's Entry of Service."

Once your spouse has been served with the petition, you may simply mail him or her copies of any papers you file later. All you need to do is sign a statement (called a *certificate of service*) that you mailed copies to your spouse. Some of the forms in this book will have a certificate of service for you to complete. If any form you file does not contain one, you will need to complete the CERTIFICATE OF SERVICE (Form 7), in appendix C of this book. To complete Form 7, type in the name of the document being sent to your spouse on the line in the main paragraph; the date you mail it on the date line; and your name and address at the bottom. Cross out either the word "Plaintiff" or "Defendant," whichever does not apply to you. Attach this form to whatever document you are sending your spouse. File one copy with the court, and keep a copy for yourself.

SETTING A COURT HEARING

You will need to set a hearing date for the temporary or final hearing, or for any preliminary matters which require a hearing (these will be discussed later in this book). The court clerk may be able to give you a date, but you will probably have to get a date from the judge's secretary. (If you don't know which judge, call the court clerk, give the clerk your case number, and ask for the name and phone number of the judge assigned to your case.) You can then either call or go see that judge's secretary and tell him you'd like to set a final hearing date for a divorce (or for whatever preliminary motion needs a hearing). Usually the judge's phone number can be found in the government section of your phone book.

The secretary may ask you how long the hearing will take. If you and your spouse have agreed on everything (an uncontested divorce), tell the secretary it is an uncontested divorce and ask for ten minutes (unless he advises you differently). If you have a contested divorce, it could take anywhere from thirty minutes to several days, depending upon such things as what matters you disagree about and how many witnesses will testify. One general rule of thumb is that the more time you need for a hearing, the longer it will take to get the hearing. Also, it is better to over-estimate the time required, rather than not schedule enough time and have to continue the hearing for several weeks. Judges do not like to go over the time scheduled! The secretary will then give you a date and time for the hearing, but you will also need to know where the hearing will be held. Ask the secretary for the location. You'll need the street address of the courthouse, as well as the room number, floor or other location within the building.

COURTROOM MANNERS

There are certain rules of procedure that are used in a court. These are really the rules of good conduct, or good manners, and are designed to keep things orderly. Many of the rules are written down, although some are unwritten customs that have just developed over many years. They aren't difficult, and most of them do make sense. Following these suggestions will make the judge respect you for your maturity and professional manner, and possibly even make him forget for a moment that you are not a lawyer. It will also increase the likelihood that you will get the things you request.

Show respect for the judge. This basically means, don't do anything to make the judge angry at you, such as arguing with him. Be polite, and call the judge "Your Honor" when you speak to him, such as "Yes, Your Honor," or "Your Honor, I brought proof of my income." Although many lawyers address judges as "Judge," this is not proper. Many of the following rules also relate to showing respect for the court. This also means wearing appropriate clothing, such as a coat and tie for men and a dress for women.

Whenever the judge talks, you listen. Even if the judge interrupts you, stop talking immediately and listen.

Only one person can talk at a time. Each person is allotted his or her own time to talk in court. The judge can only listen to one person at a time, so don't interrupt your spouse when it's his or her turn. And as difficult as it may be, stop talking if your spouse interrupts you. (Let the judge tell your spouse to keep quiet and let you have your say.)

Talk to the judge, not to your spouse. Many people get in front of a judge and begin arguing with each other. They actually turn away from the judge, face each other, and begin arguing as if they are in the room alone. This generally has several negative results: The judge can't understand what either one is saying since they both start talking at once, they both look like fools for losing control, and the judge gets angry with both of them. So whenever you speak in a courtroom, look only at the judge. Try to pretend that your spouse isn't there. Remember, you are there to convince the judge that you should have certain things. You don't need to convince your spouse.

Talk only when it's your turn. The usual procedure is for you to present your case first. When you are done saying all you came to say, your spouse will have a chance to say whatever he or she came to say. Let your spouse have his or her say. When he or she is finished you will get another chance to respond to what has been said.

Stick to the subject. Many people cannot resist the temptation to get off the track and start telling the judge all the problems with their marriage over the past twenty years. This just wastes time, and aggravates the judge. So stick to the subject, and answer the judge's questions simply and to the point.

Keep calm. Judges like things to go smoothly in their courtrooms. They don't like shouting, name calling, crying, or other displays of emotion. Generally, judges don't like family law cases because they get too emotionally charged. So give your judge a pleasant surprise by keeping calm and focusing on the issues.

Show respect for your spouse. Even if you don't respect your spouse, act like you do. All you have to do is refer to your spouse as "Mr. Smith" or "Ms. Smith." (using his or her correct name, of course).

UNCONTESTED DIVORCE 6

This chapter will provide an explanation of the uncontested divorce procedure. The following chapter will discuss the contested divorce procedure. Remember that this chapter assumes you have prepared the papers discussed in chapter 5 regarding notifying your spouse. What we are now preparing are the documents stating what you want to do.

CONTESTED OR UNCONTESTED DIVORCE?

Most lawyers have had the following experience: A new client comes in, saying she wants to file for divorce. She has discussed it with her husband, and it will be a "simple, uncontested" divorce. Once the papers are filed the husband and wife begin arguing over a few items of property. The lawyer then spends a lot of time negotiating with the husband. After much arguing, an agreement is finally reached. The case will proceed in the court as "uncontested," but only after a lot of contesting out of court. For purposes of this book, a *contested* case is one where you and your spouse will be doing your arguing in court, and leaving the decision up to the judge. An *uncontested* case is one where you will do your arguing and deciding before court, and the judge will only be approving your decision.

You probably won't know if you are going to have a contested case until you try the uncontested route and fail. Therefore, the following sections are presented mostly to assist you in attempting the uncontested case. Chapter 7 specifically discusses the contested case.

There are actually two ways that a case can be considered uncontested. The first is where you have your spouse served and he or she does not respond. The other is where you and your spouse reach an agreement on every issue in the divorce. To be in this situation you must be in agreement on the following points:

☛ How your property is to be divided.

☛ How your debts are to be divided.

☛ Which of you will have custody of the children.

☛ How much child support is to be paid by the person not having custody.

☛ Whether any alimony is to be paid, and if so, how much and for how long a period of time.

FORMS   To begin an uncontested case, the following forms should be filed with the court clerk in all cases (see chapter 5 for filing instructions):

❏ CIVIL CASE INITIATION FORM (Form 9).

❏ DISCLOSURE STATEMENT (Form 8).

❏ PETITION FOR DIVORCE (Form 11).

❏ REPORT OF DIVORCE, ANNULMENT OR DISSOLUTION OF MARRIAGE (Form 24).

❏ SHERIFF'S ENTRY OF SERVICE (Form 5), or ACKNOWLEDGMENT OF SERVICE AND CONSENT TO JURISDICTION (Form 23).

Other forms that you determine to be necessary may also be filed, either with your PETITION FOR DIVORCE or at any time before the final hearing, depending upon your situation.

The following forms will be prepared in advance, but will not be filed until the final hearing:

- ❏ FINAL JUDGMENT AND DECREE (Form 16).
- ❏ CIVIL CASE DISPOSITION FORM (Form 10).
- ❏ AGREEMENT (Form 13).

Once all of the necessary forms have been filed, you will need to call the judge's secretary to arrange for a hearing date for the final judgment (see chapter 5 regarding setting a hearing). You should tell the secretary that you need to schedule a "final hearing for an uncontested divorce." Such a hearing should not usually take more than ten minutes. See chapter 9 for information on how to handle the final hearing. The following sections give instructions for when you need each form, and how to complete it.

DISCLOSURE STATEMENT

To complete the DISCLOSURE STATEMENT (Form 8), simply type your name as Plaintiff, and your spouse's as Defendant in the upper right hand corner. If you have an AGREEMENT (Form 13) already prepared, check line #2, "Divorce with Agreement Attached." If you have not yet prepared your AGREEMENT, check line #1, "Divorce Without Agreement Attached."

CIVIL CASE INITIATION FORM

The CIVIL CASE INITIATION FORM (Form 9) must be completed in all cases. This one is easy! Fill in the county in the upper left hand corner, your name and address as the Plaintiff, and your spouse's name and address as the Defendant. In the part of the form designated "CAUSE

OF ACTION" you will check the box for "Divorce/Alimony." The Clerk will fill out the other blanks.

PETITION FOR DIVORCE

The PETITION FOR DIVORCE (Form 11) must be completed in all cases. The PETITION FOR DIVORCE is simply the paper you file with the court to begin your case and to ask the judge to give you a divorce. The PETITION FOR DIVORCE must be accompanied by your DOMESTIC RELATIONS FINANCIAL AFFIDAVIT (Form 12), which gives the judge part of the financial information he will need. The PETITION FOR DIVORCE may also be accompanied by other affidavits, depending upon your situation. Together, these papers give the judge an idea of what your situation is, and of what you want him to do.

To complete your PETITION FOR DIVORCE (Form 11):

1. Complete the top portion of the form according to the instructions in chapter 5.

2. In paragraph 1, type your name after the word "Plaintiff," and the county name.

3. In paragraph 2, check the first box if your spouse has signed an ACKNOWLEDGMENT OF SERVICE AND CONSENT TO JURISDICTION (Form 23). Check the second box if your spouse will not sign Form 23 and must be served by the sheriff. Type in your spouse's name after "Defendant." If you are going to require Sheriff's service, type in your spouse's address.

4. In paragraph 3, type the date of your marriage, and the date of separation.

5. In paragraph 4, if you have no children, check the first box. If you have children, check the second box, and identify the children by name, age, and date of birth. If you have children, you

will also need to fill in the employer and income information for you and your spouse. If you have children, be sure to include an AFFIDAVIT REGARDING CUSTODY (Form 14), which is explained more later in this chapter.

6. Paragraph 5 is for you to indicate how your marital assets and debts are to be treated. If you have prepared an AGREEMENT (Form 13), or have no undivided marital assets, check the first box. If you need the judge to distribute the assets, check the second box, and the box in that paragraph before the phrase "An equitable division of the assets and liabilities of the parties." Also, check the second box if any of the matters in that paragraph need to be decided in your case, and check the box or boxes for any of the matters that apply. If you and your spouse have not agreed upon the division of your marital assets and debts, you will need to read chapter 8 about contested divorce procedures.

7. Paragraph 6 is where you indicate the reason you want a divorce. In an uncontested case, you will use the language found in this paragraph. In a contested case, you may refer to the "fault" grounds previously discussed.

8. Paragraph 7 is where the Wife can request the restoration of her maiden name. Some judges require that if the husband files for divorce, the wife can only get her maiden name restored if she files an ANSWER AND COUNTERCLAIM (Form 15). **Warning: Do not use Form 15 in a contested divorce case!**

9. At the bottom of the last page, type in your name, address, and telephone number under the heading "Name and address." Do not sign the form yet.

10. Complete the Verification page: type in the name of the county where you will sign the PETITION FOR DIVORCE after the words "COUNTY OF," and your name on the line in the main paragraph.

11. Take this form to a notary and sign it before the notary on the line marked "Plaintiff, Pro Se."

Your PETITION FOR DIVORCE is now ready for filing. If your spouse needs to be served by the sheriff, be sure to prepare the SUMMONS (Form 4) to go along with your PETITION FOR DIVORCE (see chapter 5).

AGREEMENT

The AGREEMENT (Form 13) is used if you and your spouse can agree on the division of your property. This form includes provisions for agreements on child support and custody, alimony, and attorneys fees. Whether you and your spouse agreed on everything from the start, or whether you've gone through extensive negotiations to reach an agreement, you need to put your agreement in writing. This is done through a settlement agreement. Even if you don't agree on everything, you should put what you do agree on into a written agreement.

To complete your AGREEMENT (Form 13) you need to:

1. Complete the top portion according to the instructions in chapter 5.

2. Type in the date you were married and date you were separated on the lines in the first two paragraphs beginning with the word "WHEREAS."

3. In each section there are choices for you to make regarding your personal circumstances. Choose the provision that applies to your situation. Read through each one and look for places where you need to check a box or type in information to fit your situation.

4. In the section on CHILD CUSTODY & VISITATION, check the first box if there are no minor children. Check the second box if one of you will have custody, and check the box for which of you

(Plaintiff or Defendant) will have custody. Check the third box if you and your spouse will have joint custody, and check the box for which of you will provide the children's primary residence. Any special arrangements you wish to include can be typed in by the last box in this section.

5. If there are no minor children, check the first box in the section on CHILD SUPPORT. If there are children, check the second box and type in the amount and payment period, such as "$583.20" per "month." This amount must fall within the guidelines found in the CHILD SUPPORT GUIDELINES WORKSHEET (Form 3, Schedule A).

6. In the section on ALIMONY, check the first box if you and your spouse agree that neither of you will pay alimony. If alimony is to be paid, check the second box and complete that paragraph by also checking a box for who is to pay alimony, and filling in an amount, payment period, and when alimony will end.

7. For the section on DIVISION OF PROPERTY, check the appropriate box or boxes which describe your situation. This form assumes that you and your spouse have already divided most personal items. This is much easier than trying to cover all items in the AGREEMENT. If you and your spouse are living separately, just be sure that you each have the personal property and household goods you each want, and that you have separate bank accounts. If you are still living in the same household, get separate bank accounts, and make a list of the items each of you will get when one or both of you moves out. The following subcategories will require you to fill in additional information:

   a. Real property. If you do not own any real property, check the box for the first paragraph. If you have real property that one of you will keep, check the second box. You will need to fill in the name of the county where the property is located and the address of the property. The remaining blanks are to fill in either the word "Plaintiff" or "Defendant," whichever reflects your agreement. The person who will give up the property is the one who will execute a *quit claim deed*. The third box is for the situation where you agree to sell the property and divide the proceeds. Unless one of you can pay-off the other, or get a mortgage to do so, sale may be the only other option.

b. Automobiles, boats, etc. This paragraph is to clearly identify which car each of you will keep. In the first blank fill in the year, make, and model of the car the plaintiff will keep. Then fill in the "VIN#." This is the Vehicle Identification Number, which can be found on the vehicle and also on the vehicle registration certificate. The third and fourth blanks are for the same information regarding the vehicle the defendant will keep. For any other vehicle, such as a boat, RV, motorcycle, etc., be sure to transfer the title into the name of the person who will keep it before signing the AGREEMENT. (Or you can modify the AGREEMENT to include other vehicles in the same manner as the cars.)

8. In the section on INSURANCE, check the box or boxes that reflect your agreement. The judge will probably be looking for some provision for medical insurance for any minor children.

9. In the section on DEBTS, you will need to indicate which debts are to be each person's responsibility. Keep in mind that if this agreement only affects responsibility for debts as between you and your spouse. For example, suppose you have a car loan which is in both names. Your agreement says your spouse is to keep that car and be responsible for paying the loan. If your spouse doesn't pay, the bank can still come after you for payment. You would then have to take your spouse back to court for violating your agreement.

10. The section on TAXES requires you to decide how you and your spouse will handle your income tax matters. The third paragraph simply follows federal law on this matter. The following information will help you complete this section:

   a. Joint or individual return. You must file individual returns for the year in which your final judgment is entered. However, if you are getting divorced early in the year and before you have filed your tax return for the previous year, you will need to check the box for the first paragraph to indicate whether you will file a joint return or individual returns for that year. Which way you file should be determined by such factors as whether you will save money by filing a joint return, whether you can trust your spouse to cooperate so you get your share of any refund, and whether your spouse's business dealings will increase your chances of an audit and penalties. Any refund check will require both of your signatures to cash, so you had better be sure that your spouse won't try to keep the entire refund by getting your signature then cashing the check, or by refusing to sign the check thereby preventing either of you from getting it. Also, if your spouse is self-employed, or has a habit of putting false information on tax returns, you would be liable for any interest and penalty charges in the event of an audit.

   b. Responsibility for taxes. The second paragraph is for the situation where taxes will, or may be, owed. Again, only check this box if you still need to file your return for the year prior to the year in which your final judgment will be entered. Simply check the box for who will be responsible to any tax which may be owed, and fill in the applicable year.

11. Each of you must sign and date the AGREEMENT before a notary public where indicated at the bottom, then file it with the clerk.

Form 13 is a basic form, which can be changed as needed to fit your situation and desires. You can either write in special provisions in Form 13 itself, or type up your own settlement agreement using Form 13 and the following examples as guidelines. A very important goal when writing your own settlement agreement provisions is to be clear and precise. *Be sure to read the entire agreement carefully before signing.* If there are any provisions you do not understand, or if there are special provisions needed which are not included (unless you feel comfortable modifying the AGREEMENT to include them), you should consult an attorney.

Sample Optional Custody Provisions

There is no end to the possible variations of custody arrangements. The following are examples of custody provisions for you to consider.

Example 1

SOLE CUSTODY

Sole Custody. The Plaintiff shall have temporary and permanent custody and control of the minor child(ren) being issue of this marriage, to wit: _____ *{type in names of children}*, and shall be denominated as the "Custodial Parent." The Defendant shall have the right of reasonable and liberal visitation with the children at times and places to be agreed upon by the parties, and shall be denominated as the "Non-Custodial Parent." Should the parties be unable to agree upon reasonable visitation, the Defendant shall be entitled to visitation as follows: _____ *{type in an agreed-upon visitation schedule—see the following sample visitation provisions}.*

Example 2

JOINT CUSTODY

Joint Custody. The Plaintiff and Defendant shall share "Joint Custody" of the minor child(ren), to wit: _____ *{type in names of children}.* It is the intention of the parties in agreeing to this custodial arrangement that each of them shall have a full and active role in providing a sound moral, social, economic, religious, and educational environment for the child(ren). The parents shall consult with one another in substantial questions relating to religious upbringing, educational programs, significant changes in social environment, and non-emergency health care of the child(ren). In accepting the grant of privileges conferred by this custodial arrangement upon each of the parents, they specifically recognize that these powers shall not be exercised for the purpose of frustrating, denying, or controlling in any manner, the social development of the other parent. The parents shall exert their best efforts to work cooperatively in future plans consistent with the best interest of the child(ren) and in amicably resolving such disputes as may arise. For purposes of legal definition, the Wife shall have final decision making authority and shall be considered to have primary physical custody of the child(ren), and the Husband shall be denominated as having secondary physical custody.

Sample Optional Visitation Provisions

There is no end to the possible variations of visitation arrangements. The following are examples of visitation provisions for you to consider.

Example 1

VISITATION
DURING
INFANCY

Visitation During Infancy. Until such time as the child(ren) shall have attained the child(ren)'s third birthday, all visitation will be at the residence of the Custodial Parent, subject to the following schedule: during the first and third weekends of each month from Saturday at 9:00 a.m. to 5:00 p.m. and Sunday from 1:00 p.m. to 5:00 p.m. provided the Non-Custodial Parent shall give the Custodial Parent at least 24 hours advance notice, written or oral, of any intention to exercise this right.

Example 2

Visitation After Infancy. After the child(ren) has attained the child(ren)'s third birthday, the visitation of the Non-Custodial Parent shall be at such place of his or her choice, and such visitation shall be reasonable and liberal, but in the event that the parties are unable to agree to such visitation the agreed upon schedule shall be as follows:

(a)   During the first and third weekends of each month from Friday at 6:00 p.m. until Sunday at 6:00 p.m. provided that the Non-Custodial Parent shall give the Custodial Parent at least 24 hours advance notice, written or oral, of any intention not to exercise this right;

(b)   For any _____ weeks during summer vacation so long as the Non-Custodial Parent does not interfere with or interrupt any of the child's school and further provided that the Non-Custodial Parent shall give the Custodial Parent at least (14) days advance notice, written or oral, of each summer visitation;

(c)   During even-number years, the Thanksgiving holiday, from 6:00 p.m. on the Wednesday before Thanksgiving to 6:00 p.m. on the Sunday following Thanksgiving, and the New Years holiday from December 27, at 6:00 p.m. to January 1, at 6:00 p.m., provided that the Non-Custodial Parent shall give the Custodial Parent at least 14 days advance notice of each intended visitation;

(d)   During odd-numbered years, the Christmas holiday from December 23, at 6:00 p.m. to December 27, at 6:00 p.m; the spring vacation specified by the child's school district, from the first day at 6:00 p.m. to the 7th day at 6:00 p.m. (the Custodial Parent shall give the Non-Custodial Parent 30 days notice as to the specified dates of the spring vacation); and the child(ren)'s birthdays, from 6:00 p.m. of the day preceding until 6:00 p.m. of birthday; all provided that the Non-Custodial Parent shall give the Custodial Parent 14 days advance notice of each intended visitation;

(e)   The Non-Custodial Parent shall be responsible for transportation and promptness in each visitation. For each visitation, the Non-Custodial Parent shall receive the child(ren) at the residence of the Custodial Parent, and after such visitation, shall return the child to the residence of the Custodial Parent.

Example 3

VISITATION WITH GEOGRAPHICAL SEPARATION

Visitation in the Event of Geographical Separation. Notwithstanding the aforementioned, should the parties be domiciled more than one hundred miles apart, and the minor child be above the age of three years, the following minimum visitation shall apply:

(a)   The Non-Custodial Parent shall be entitled to _____ days regular visitation per month. In no event shall the monthly visitation be cumulative, nor shall the regular visitation in any one month exceed _____ consecutive hours.

(b)   In addition, the Non-Custodial Parent shall be entitled to _____ weeks of visitation to take place during the Summer, or contemporaneously with the child's vacation, that may be exercised during any calendar year. The purpose of this visitation is to allow the Non-Custodial Parent extended time with the minor child. This vacation visitation shall not exceed _____ consecutive days per visit, and shall be in lieu of the regular visitation for the months in which vacation visitation is exercised. In the event that vacation visitation bridges two months, it shall be in lieu of the regular visitation for both months.

(c)   The Non-Custodial Parent shall be responsible for the expenses of transporting the minor child to the residence of the Non-Custodial Parent and the Custodial Parent shall be responsible for the expenses of returning the child to the residence of the Custodial Parent.

Example 4

VISITATION AND MORALS

Although the parties are establishing for minimum visitation, it is the intention of the parties that either shall enjoy the right of reasonable and liberal visitation with said child(ren) at times and places to be agreed upon by the parties. Both parties agree to maintain a wholesome environment for the chid(ren) and covenant to not expose the child(ren) to illegal controlled substances, nor to excessive alcoholic consumption on the part of themselves or any guests, nor to immoral practices, including, but not limited to, intimate and/or overnight associations with members of the opposite sex during periods of visitation. Violations of these conditions shall be grounds for the non-violating party to ask the court for restrictions upon such visitation and shall entitle the non-violating party to such costs and fees incurred.

Sample Optional Child Support Provisions

The following are examples of optional child support provisions for you to consider.

Example 1

CHILD SUPPORT ANNUAL REVIEW AND ADJUSTMENT

Child Support Annual Review and Adjustment. On the first anniversary of the date of this Agreement, and continuing with each successive anniversary date, the Non-Custodial Parent shall provide to the Custodial parent a copy of his or her W-2, state, and federal returns for the previous year. The Non-Custodial Parent's total gross annual income for the previous year shall then be determined from the aforementioned information, and multiplied by _____% (as the applicable percentage of child support contribution), then divided by twelve, to obtain a monthly average for child support purposes. In the event this sum exceeds the original child support amounts, then the child support payments commencing thirty days from each said anniversary shall incorporate the new child support amounts.

Example 2

CHILD SUPPORT FOR HIGHER EDUCATION

Higher Education. The parties recognize and accept an obligation to support said child(ren) in pursuit of a college education. Therefore, each of the parties agrees to pay a pro-rata share of the reasonable college tuition and room and board expenses for the child(ren), so long as said child(ren) are enrolled full-time in a course of college study at an accredited college or university in pursuit of a bachelor's degree. The pro-rata share of each of the parties shall be based upon the relative income of the parties as demonstrated by W-2, federal, and state tax documentation. The obligation created under this item shall not extend beyond the fifth year following the child(ren)'s graduation from high school nor exceed the cost of tuition for a full time in-state student enrolled in a state college within 100 miles of the residence of the custodial parent.

Example 3

CHILD SUPPORT ENFORCEMENT

Garnishment. The Non-Custodial Parent is hereby notified that, pursuant to the provisions of O.C.G.A. § 19-6-30, whenever, in violation of the terms of this order there shall have been a failure to make the support payments due hereunder so that the amount unpaid is equal to or greater than the amount payable for one month, the payments required to be made may be collected by the process of continuing garnishment for support, or income deduction order, at the election of the receiving spouse.

Affidavit Regarding Custody

The AFFIDAVIT REGARDING CUSTODY (Form 14) must be completed if you have minor children. To complete Form 14 you need to:

1. Complete the top portion according to the instructions in chapter 5.

2. In paragraph 1, type in the name, age, birthdate and present address of each child, and indicate with whom the child is living.

3. In paragraph 2, type in the addresses where each child has lived during the past five years. If a child is not yet five years old, type in the places the child has lived since birth. If the children have not lived with their parents, state with whom they have lived for the past five years, and where.

4. Paragraphs 3, 4, and 5 require you to tell whether you have been involved in any other court cases involving the custody of, or visitation with, your children; and tell if you know of any court case involving custody of, or visitation with, the children (even if you weren't involved in the case). If there are no such cases, you don't need to do anything with paragraphs 4 or 5. If there are such cases, you need to describe the other case by giving the names of the parties, the name and location of the court, and the case number.

5. Take the form to a notary, and sign it on the "Signature" line before the notary.

ANSWER AND COUNTERCLAIM FOR NAME CHANGE PURPOSES

> ***Warning: Do not use Form 15 in a contested divorce!***

The ANSWER AND COUNTERCLAIM (Form 15) is only for very special circumstances. This form should *only* be used if *all* four of the following conditions apply to your situation:

1. You and your spouse can agree on everything.

2. Both of you sign and file a settlement AGREEMENT (Form 13).

3. The husband is the Plaintiff.

4. The wife wants her maiden name restored. (However, if the wife is the Plaintiff, she may simply ask for her maiden name to be restored in her Complaint.)

To complete the ANSWER AND COUNTERCLAIM (Form 15), you need to:

1. Complete the top portion according to the instructions in chapter 5.

2. Type in your spouse's name in the blank space in the first paragraph.

3. Type in your spouse's name in paragraph 3.

4. Have your spouse sign on the "Signature" line before a notary public.

5. File this form with the clerk of the superior court within forty-five days of the filing of the PETITION FOR DIVORCE.

FINAL JUDGMENT AND DECREE

Form 16 will be used if you and your spouse have signed an Agreement. Form 17 will be used if your spouse did not respond to the Petition for Divorce, or only signed an Answer. For Form 17, see chapter 7 for instructions.

To complete the FINAL JUDGMENT AND DECREE (Form 16) you need to:

1. Complete the top portion according to the instructions in chapter 6.

2. The last (unnumbered) paragraph is for the judge to fill in the date of the judgment. The judge will do this at the hearing.

If the judge tells you to change something major in the FINAL JUDGMENT AND DECREE, you will need to make a note of exactly what changes the judge requires, or what he ordered, then go home and prepare the FINAL JUDGMENT AND DECREE the way the judge instructed. You will then need to take the revised form back to the judge for his signature.

You will also need to fill in a REPORT OF DIVORCE, ANNULMENT OR DISSOLUTION OF MARRIAGE (Form 24). You will probably be given one of these by the clerk, but if not, use Form 24 in appendix C. Just fill in the information required for each box on the form.

If you need to prepare the FINAL JUDGMENT AND DECREE after the hearing, you will also complete a CERTIFICATE OF SERVICE (Form 7), attach it to the FINAL JUDGMENT AND DECREE, and deliver it to the judge's secretary. Also give two extra copies to the secretary, along with a stamped envelope addressed to yourself and a stamped envelope addressed to your spouse. Ask the secretary whether you should sign and date the CERTIFICATE OF SERVICE. Sometimes the secretary will handle mailing the judgment after the judge signs it, in which case he or she may sign the CERTIFICATE OF SERVICE.

Contested Divorce 7

Procedure Differences from Uncontested Divorce

This book cannot turn you into a trial lawyer. It is very risky to try to handle a contested case yourself, although it has been done. There are several differences between a contested and an uncontested case. First, in an uncontested case the judge will usually go along with whatever you and your spouse have worked out. In a contested case you need to prove that you are entitled to what you are asking for. This means you will need a longer time for the hearing, you will need to present papers as evidence, and you may need to have witnesses testify for you.

Second, you may have to do some extra work to get the evidence you need, such as sending out subpoenas (which are discussed in the next section of this chapter), or even hiring a private investigator. Third, the FINAL JUDGMENT AND DECREE form will be more complicated.

Also, you will need to pay extra attention to assure that your spouse is properly notified of any court hearings, and that he or she is sent copies of any papers you file with the court clerk.

When it becomes apparent that you have a contested divorce, it is probably time to seriously consider hiring an attorney, especially if the issue of child custody is involved. If you are truly ready to go to war over custody, it shows that this is an extremely important matter for you, and you may want to get professional assistance. You probably would get professional assistance if your house needed a structural addition, or your appendix needed to be removed, or your business had some complicated accounting issues to resolve with the IRS. If the fight is too big, don't be afraid to bring in help. You can expect a contested case with near certainty when your spouse is seriously threatening to fight you every inch of the way, or when he or she hires an attorney.

On the other hand, you shouldn't assume that you need an attorney just because your spouse has hired one. Sometimes it will be easier to deal with the attorney than with your spouse. The attorney is not as emotionally involved and may see your settlement proposal as reasonable. So discuss things with your spouse's attorney first and see if things can be worked out. You can always hire your own lawyer if your spouse's isn't reasonable. Just be very cautious about signing any papers until you are certain you understand what they mean. You may want to have an attorney review any papers prepared by your spouse's lawyer before you sign them.

Aside from deciding if you want a lawyer, there are three main procedure differences between the uncontested and the contested divorce. First, you may need to prepare additional forms. Second, you will need to be more prepared for the hearing. Third, you will not prepare the FINAL JUDGMENT AND DECREE (Form 17) until after the hearing with the judge. This is because you won't know what to put in the FINAL JUDGMENT AND DECREE until the judge decides the various matters in dispute.

FORMS   To begin a contested case, the following forms should be filed with the court clerk in all cases (see chapter 5 for filing instructions):

❑ CIVIL CASE INITIATION FORM (Form 9).

❑ DISCLOSURE STATEMENT (Form 8).

❑ PETITION FOR DIVORCE (Form 11).

❑ DOMESTIC RELATIONS FINANCIAL AFFIDAVIT (Form 12).

❑ REPORT OF DIVORCE, ANNULMENT OR DISSOLUTION OF MARRIAGE (Form 24).

❑ SHERIFF'S ENTRY OF SERVICE (Form 5), or ACKNOWLEDGMENT OF SERVICE AND CONSENT TO JURISDICTION (Form 23).

The following forms will be prepared in advance, but will not be filed until the final hearing:

❑ FINAL JUDGMENT AND DECREE (Form 16).

❑ CIVIL CASE DISPOSITION FORM (Form 10).

❑ AGREEMENT (Form 13).

The instructions for preparing all of these forms, except the DOMESTIC RELATIONS FINANCIAL AFFIDAVIT (Form 12), may be found in chapter 6.

DOMESTIC RELATIONS FINANCIAL AFFIDAVIT

You and your spouse must each complete a separate DOMESTIC RELATIONS FINANCIAL AFFIDAVIT (Form 12).

Generally, monthly guidelines are most appropriate, so try to figure each of the categories on a monthly basis. If you are paid weekly, or every two weeks, you will need to convert your income to a monthly figure. The same conversion will be required for any of your expenses that are not paid monthly. To convert weekly amounts to monthly amounts, just take the weekly figure and multiply it by 4.3. (There are roughly 4.3 weeks to a month.) To convert from every two weeks, divide by 2 and then multiply by 4.3.

All you need to do is fill in all of the blank spaces on the DOMESTIC RELATIONS FINANCIAL AFFIDAVIT (Form 12), then take it to a notary public before you sign it. You will sign it before the notary, then staple it to your petition (after you have made three copies). Make a blank copy for your spouse to complete. Most of the blanks in Form 12 clearly indicate what information is to be filled in there; however, the following may answer some questions:

1. Complete the top portion of the form, by filling in your name as "Affiant" (an *affiant* is a person who signs an affidavit) and your spouse's name as "Spouse." Type in your names, ages and social security numbers. Fill in the date of your marriage, date of separation, and the number of time each of you has been married.

2. Fill in the names and dates of birth of your children.

3. Save paragraph 2 for last.

4. In paragraph 3, type in your monthly salary, then add up all of your money over and above your salary (second jobs, commissions, etc.) on the next line. If you have earned any money in any other category, fill in those blanks and add the sums up on the line in 3.A for GROSS MONTHLY INCOME. Take this total and write it on line 2(a) as well. See chapter 5 for a discussion of what constitutes gross income.

5. In paragraph 3.B, identify your benefits, if applicable to your situation. In 3.C type in your net monthly income, only excluding state and federal taxes and FICA. Take this number and write it in line 2(b). Also indicate your pay period and the number of federal exemptions you will be eligible to claim on your tax return.

6. Paragraph 4 simply asks for the items you have already identified in the PROPERTY INVENTORY (Form 1). Fill in the categories and estimate what you think the present value is for each item, and who has it. Total these figures at the bottom of the list.

7. Paragraph 5 refers to "AVERAGE MONTHLY EXPENSES." Simply refer to each item listed and estimate as best you can the amount you spend on that item in a month. If a particular item

is an annual expense, such as auto insurance, convert it to a monthly amount. (If you are just guessing, place an asterisk (*) next to the figure.) Total these items at the bottom of the paragraph. Take this total and write it on the first line in 2(c).

8. List your creditors (credit cards, car note, etc., which have not been entered previously) to complete paragraph 5.B. Write this number on the second line on 2(c). Add 5.A. and 5.B. together for 5.C. Write this number in the final line of 2(c).

9. Now go back to paragraph 2. Subtract the last line of 2(c) from line 2(b) and write the answer in line 2(d). (That is, subtract the "Total monthly expenses and payments to creditors" from the "Net monthly income.")

10. The last calculation, for line 2(e), requires you to go back to Form 3 and calculate the guideline child support as a monthly amount. Write this monthly amount in 2(e). See the CHILD SUPPORT GUIDELINES WORKSHEET (Form 3).

11. Take Form 12 to a notary public and sign it before the notary on the line designated "Affiant." The notary will complete the part of the form directly opposite your signature.

If your spouse does not have a copy of this information, you will need to send him or her a copy. You will also need to complete a CERTIFICATE OF SERVICE (Form 7). On the CERTIFICATE OF SERVICE, fill in the name of the document as "Domestic Relations Financial Affidavit."

COLLECTING INFORMATION

The judge will require a DOMESTIC RELATIONS FINANCIAL AFFIDAVIT (Form 12) from you, and also one from your spouse. If your spouse has indicated that he or she will not cooperate at all, and will not provide a DOMESTIC RELATIONS FINANCIAL AFFIDAVIT, you may have to try to get the information yourself. You should first try to file a REQUEST FOR PRODUCTION OF DOCUMENTS (Form 18).

REQUEST FOR PRODUCTION OF DOCUMENTS

The generally preferred practice, before you subpoena documents is called a REQUEST FOR PRODUCTION OF DOCUMENTS (Form 18). To complete Form 18 you need to:

1. Complete the top portion according to the instructions in chapter 5.

2. Type your spouse's name and address (or whoever you are requesting documents from) after the word "TO:"

3. In the main paragraph, cross out either the word "Plaintiff" or "Defendant," whichever does not apply to you.

4. In the main paragraph, type in your address in the blank space.

5. In the space after the main paragraph, describe the documents or information you want. Examples are:

    ☛ "All documents relating to _____."

    ☛ "Copies of any checks issued with respect to _____ _____."

    ☛ "All documents related to the payment of _____ to _____."

    ☛ "All payroll records indicating the annual, and year-to-date income of _____."

6. Fill in the date, sign your name on the last line, and type your name, address, and phone number below it. Also, below the signature line, cross out either the word "Plaintiff" or "Defendant," whichever applies to you.

SUBPOENAS

If your spouse refuses to cooperate, it may speed things up if you are able to get the information yourself, and have it available at the hearing. This will require you to have subpoenas issued. To get a subpoena, go to the Superior Court Clerk's office and ask for one. They cost about $1.00 each, more or less, depending upon the county.

Before you send a subpoena to your spouse's employer, or bank, or accountant, you probably should let your spouse know what you are about to do. The thought that you are about to get these other people involved in your divorce may be enough to get your spouse to cooperate. If your spouse calls and says "I'll give you the information," give him or her a few days to follow through. Ask when you can expect to receive the DOMESTIC RELATIONS FINANCIAL AFFIDAVIT, and offer to send your spouse another blank copy if he or she needs one.

If your spouse sends a completed DOMESTIC RELATIONS FINANCIAL AFFIDAVIT, don't send the subpoena. If your spouse doesn't follow through, go ahead with the subpoena. You can send subpoenas to as many people or organizations as you need, but you'll need to use the following procedure for each subpoena. If you were able to do a good job making copies of important papers while preparing to file for divorce, you should have the information you need to figure out where you need to send subpoenas. Your spouse's income information can be obtained from his or her employer. Stock and bond information can be obtained from his or her stock broker, bank account balances from the bank, auto loan balances from the lender, etc.

You can have subpoenas issued to any or all of these places, but don't overdo it. Concentrate on income information (especially if you are asking for child support or expect to pay child support), and information on the major property items. And, it may not be necessary to send out subpoenas if you already have recent copies of the papers relating to these items. You can always show the judge the copies of your spouse's paystubs, W-2 tax statements, or other papers at the hearing.

Fill out the subpoena (which you obtained from the court clerk), just as you have filled out other documents in your divorce. You are probably the Plaintiff, and you now know the Court. Identify in the subpoena what documents you want to have. Next, have the sheriff, or a process server, personally serve the subpoena to the person or place named in the subpoena. The sheriff will need at least one extra copy of the subpoena, and a check for the service fee. The employer, bank, etc., should send you the requested information.

If the employer calls you and says that you must pay for copies, ask him or her how much they will cost and send a check or money order (if the amount isn't too high and you don't already have some fairly recent income information). If the employer doesn't provide the information, you can try sending a letter to the employer saying: "unless you provide the information requested in the subpoena in seven days, a motion for contempt will be filed with the circuit court." This may scare the employer into sending you the information.

The sheriff, or process server, will have also filed an affidavit verifying when the subpoena was served. There are more procedures you could go through to force the employer to give the information, but it probably isn't worth the hassle and you'd probably need an attorney to help you with it. At the final hearing you can tell the judge that your spouse refused to provide income information, and that the subpoena was not honored by the employer. The judge may do something to help you out, or he may advise you to see a lawyer.

There is also a procedure where you send written questions to your spouse, which he or she must answer in writing and under oath. These written questions are called *interrogatories*. If your spouse did not file a DOMESTIC RELATIONS FINANCIAL AFFIDAVIT, he or she probably will not answer the interrogatories either, which would leave you no better off. However, if you would like to try this, you may be able to locate the two forms you would need ("Plaintiff's First Interrogatories" and "Plaintiff's First Request for Production and Notice to Produce") at a law library in a forms book.

Once you collect the information needed, you can prepare for the hearing.

PROPERTY AND DEBTS

Generally, the judge will look at your property and debts, and will try to divide them "fairly." This does not mean they will necessarily be divided fifty-fifty. What you want to do is offer the judge a reasonable solution that looks fair. Adultery or other misconduct on the part of one party may be used to justify an unequal division of property and debts.

It's time to review the PROPERTY INVENTORY (Form 1) and the DEBT INVENTORY (Form 2) you prepared earlier. For each item of property, note which of the following categories it fits into (it may fit into more than one):

1. You really want.

2. You'd like to have.

3. You don't care either way.

4. Your spouse really wants.

5. Your spouse would like to have.

6. Your spouse doesn't care either way.

Now start a list of what each of you should end up with, using the categories listed above. You will eventually end up with a list of things you can probably get with little difficulty (you really want and your spouse doesn't care), those which you'll fight over (you both really want), and those which need to be divided but can probably be easily divided equally (you both don't really care).

At the hearing the judge will probably try to get you to work out your disagreements, but he won't put up with arguing for very long. In the end he will arbitrarily divide the items you can't agree upon, or he may order you to sell those items and divide the money you get equally. A judge will not decide ownership of each pot and pan!

On the few items that are really important to you it may be necessary for you to try to prove why you should get them. It will help if you can convince the judge of one or more of the following:

1. You paid for the item out of your own earnings or funds.

2. You are the one who primarily uses that item.

3. You use the item in your employment, business, or hobby.

4. You are willing to give up something else you really want in exchange for that item. (Of course you will try to give up something from your "don't care" or your "like to have" list.)

5. The item is needed for your children (assuming you will have custody).

Make up a list of how you think the property should be divided. And make it a reasonably fair and equal list, regardless of how angry you are at your spouse. Even if the judge changes some of it to appear fair to your spouse, you will most likely get more of what you want than if you don't offer a suggestion. (No, this is not an exception to the negotiating rule of letting your spouse make the first offer, because at this point you are no longer just negotiating with your spouse. You are now negotiating with the judge. At this point you are trying to impress the judge with your fairness; not trying to convince your spouse.)

MARITAL AND NON-MARITAL PROPERTY

Special problems arise if a claim of nonmarital property becomes an issue. This may be in terms of your spouse trying to get your nonmarital property, or you trying to get property you feel your spouse is wrongly claiming to be nonmarital. Basically, nonmarital property is property either of you had before you were married, and kept separate.

Not every dime in the marriage is subject to division. If one party has received an inheritance, and kept the inheritance completely separate, it may qualify as nonmarital property. Likewise, some future interests in business and property can be nonmarital. These rules are complex and may be worth a discussion with personal counsel. It is also a good idea to have any papers that prove the property you claim as nonmarital property is actually nonmarital property. These would be papers showing that:

- ☞ You bought the item before you were married (such as dated sales receipts).

- ☞ You inherited the item as your own property (such as certified copies of wills and probate court papers).

- ☞ You got the property by exchanging it for property you had before you got married, or for property you received as a gift or through an inheritance (such as a statement from the person you made the exchange with, or some kind of receipt showing what was exchanged).

If you want to get at assets your spouse is claiming are nonmarital assets, you will need to collect the following types of evidence:

- ☞ Papers showing that you helped pay for the asset (such as a check that you wrote, or bank statements showing that your money went into the same account that was used to make payments on the asset). For example, suppose your spouse purchased a house before you got married. During your marriage you made some of the mortgage payments with your own checking account (you will have cancelled checks, hopefully with the mortgage account number on them, to prove this). At other times, you deposited some of your paychecks into your spouse's checking account, and your spouse wrote checks from that account to pay the mortgage (again, there should be some bank records and cancelled checks to show that this was done). Since you contributed to the purchase of the house, you can claim some of the value of the house as a marital asset.

- ☞ Papers showing you paid for repairs of the asset. If you paid for repairs on a home or car your spouse had before you were married, you can claim part of the value.

☛ Papers showing that the asset was improved, or increased in value during your marriage. Example 1: Your spouse owned the house before you were married. During your marriage you and your spouse added a family room to the house. This may enable you to make a claim for some of the value of the house. Example 2: Your spouse owned the house before you were married. The day before you got married, the house was worth $85,000. Now the house is appraised at $115,000. You could claim part of the $30,000 of increased value.

FINAL
JUDGMENT AND
DECREE

During the hearing the judge will announce who gets which items. Make a list of this as the judge tells you. Then, complete the FINAL JUDGMENT AND DECREE (Form 17) according to what the judge says. Once you have completed the FINAL JUDGMENT AND DECREE, make a copy and send it to your spouse. Send the original to the judge (not the court clerk), along with a completed CERTIFICATE OF SERVICE (Form 7) stapled to it showing the date you sent a copy to your spouse. If your spouse doesn't object to how you've prepared the FINAL JUDGMENT AND DECREE, the judge will sign the judgment and return a copy to you. You should send the judge the original and two copies of the FINAL JUDGMENT AND DECREE, along with two stamped envelopes (one addressed to yourself, and the other addressed to your spouse).

CHILD CUSTODY AND VISITATION

Generally, if you are the wife, the odds start out in favor of you getting custody. But don't depend upon the odds. Start out by reviewing the various factors the judge may consider in deciding the custody question. These can be found in chapter 5. For each item listed in that section, write down an explanation of how that item applies to you. This will be your argument when you have your hearing with the judge.

Many custody battles revolve around the moral fitness of one or both of the parents. If you become involved in this type of a custody fight, you should consult a lawyer. Charges of moral unfitness (such as illegal drug use, child abuse, immoral sexual conduct) can require long court hearings involving the testimony of many witnesses, as well as possibly the employment of private investigators. For such a hearing you will require the help of an attorney who knows the law, what questions to ask witnesses, and the rules of evidence.

If the only question is whether you or your spouse have been the main caretaker of the child, you can always have a friend, neighbor, or relative come into the hearing (if they are willing to help you out) to testify on your behalf. Then it may not be necessary for you to have an attorney. But, if you need to subpoena an unwilling witness to testify, you should have an attorney.

The judge's decision regarding custody will have to be put into the FINAL JUDGMENT AND DECREE (Form 17), but it will be more involved. Read chapter 7 for instructions on preparing the FINAL JUDGMENT AND DECREE.

CHILD SUPPORT

In Georgia, as in most states, the question of child support is mostly a matter of a mathematical calculation. Getting a fair child support amount depends upon the accuracy of the income information presented to the judge. If you feel fairly sure that the information your spouse presents is accurate, or that you have obtained accurate information about his or her income, there isn't much to argue about. The judge will take the income information provided, use the formula to calculate the amount to be paid, and order that amount to be paid.

In most cases, there won't be much room to argue about the amount, so there usually isn't a need to get an attorney. If you claim your spouse has not provided accurate income information, it will be up to you to prove this to the judge by showing the income information you have obtained from your spouse's employer or other source of income.

The only areas open for argument are whatever special needs are claimed by the party asking for child support. Once again, it will be necessary for that party to provide proof of the cost of these special needs by producing billing statements, receipts, or other papers to show the amount of these needs. The judge's decision regarding child support will have to be put into the FINAL JUDGMENT AND DECREE as well.

ALIMONY

A dispute over alimony may require a lawyer, especially if there is a request for permanent alimony because of a disability. Such a claim may require the testimony of expert witnesses (such as doctors, accountants, and actuaries), which requires the special skills of an attorney to present the case. A charge of adultery may also require a lawyer and possibly a private investigator as well. These alimony factors will be the subject of the court hearing on this question. You should determine what information (including papers and the testimony of witnesses) you will need to present to the judge to either support or refute the reasons alimony was requested.

For temporary (also called *rehabilitative*) alimony, the most common reason is that the person needs help until he or she can get training to enter the work force. The questions that will need to be answered are:

1. What has the person been trained for in the past?

2. What type of training is needed before the person can again be employable in that field?

3. How long will this training take?

4. What amount of income can be expected upon employment?

5. How much money is required for the training?

Questions which may be asked in either a temporary or a permanent alimony situation include an examination of the situation of the parties during their marriage that led to the person not working, what contribution to the marriage that person made, and what improper conduct on the part of the other party makes an award of alimony appropriate. You should be prepared to present evidence regarding these questions.

TEMPORARY HEARING

In a contested case, the first hearing will be a temporary hearing. In many cases, however, the temporary hearing reflects what the judge would be inclined to do in a final hearing. If the judge has all of the information available at the temporary hearing, there is little point in coming back to argue the same points all over again. Therefore, it is common to have the temporary order stand as the FINAL JUDGMENT AND DECREE. If this is the case, refer to the next section. However, if you think a temporary order may be entered, a TEMPORARY ORDER (Form 25) is provided in appendix C. It will be handled the same as the FINAL JUDGMENT AND DECREE.

FINAL JUDGMENT AND DECREE

In a contested divorce, it is not possible to use the same FINAL JUDGMENT AND DECREE form as in an uncontested divorce. It is very likely that the judge will either prepare the Final Judgment him or herself; direct his or her clerk to prepare it; or appoint a lawyer to prepare it. However, you should be prepared to offer a FINAL JUDGMENT AND DECREE form to the judge at the hearing. Form 17 in appendix C is for this purpose. You should complete as much of the FINAL JUDGMENT AND DECREE (Form 17) as possible before the hearing. The FINAL JUDGMENT AND DECREE form is designed so that you can complete it at the hearing according to what the judge decides on each issue. You can complete ahead of time any items that you and your spouse have agreed upon.

You should give your spouse a copy of the FINAL JUDGMENT AND DECREE before the hearing so that he or she can tell the judge that he or she is aware of what it says, and agrees with it.

To complete the FINAL JUDGMENT AND DECREE (Form 17) you need to:

1. Complete the top portion according to the instructions in chapter 5.

2. Check the box before each of the paragraphs numbered 1 through 12 that apply to your situation, according to the following guidelines. If a paragraph or provision does not apply to your situation, simply leave it blank.

3. Paragraph 1: Check the box if the wife will have her former name restored, and type her restored name in the blank.

4. Paragraph 2: Type in each child's name, date of birth, and either the word "Husband" or "Wife" depending upon which one will take custody of that child.

5. Paragraph 3: Check the box for "Husband" or "Wife," whichever one will be paying child support. Type in the amount of the support payment, how often it will be paid (weekly, monthly, etc.), and the date the first payment is due. If the amounts are outside of the guidelines on page 152, check the appropriate box to explain why.

6. Paragraph 4: Check either "Husband" or "Wife," whichever will be responsible for health insurance for the children.

7. Paragraph 5: Check the box for "Husband" or "Wife," whichever one will be paying alimony. Type in the amount of the alimony payment, how often it will be paid (weekly, monthly, etc.), the date the first payment is due, and check the appropriate boxes to indicate when alimony will end. The first box has a blank in which to type the date the alimony payments will end, in the event temporary alimony is awarded. The second box designates

permanent alimony. The law in many states requires the judgment to give the reasons why alimony is or is not awarded. The third box is for when you and your spouse have agreed on the question of alimony, so just check the appropriate box. The fourth box is for when the judge decides this question. You will need to type in, or write in, the judge's reasons.

8. Paragraph 6: This paragraph is for the amount of attorney's fees (if any are to be paid by either party), the name of the attorney to be paid, the amount of court costs awarded, and the number of days in which these amounts must be paid.

9. Paragraphs 7, 8, 9, and 10 are to cover the division of your property and debts. If these are the same items covered in your settlement agreement, you can leave these paragraphs blank, because they are already covered in paragraph 1 of this form. These paragraphs will be used when you do not have a settlement agreement, and the judge has decided who will get what assets and who will pay what debts.

10. Paragraph 11: If there is a dispute as to what nonmarital assets and debts belong to you and your spouse, you will need to complete this paragraph after the judge has decided this question.

11. Paragraph 12: This is a space to write in any other agreements, or orders.

12. The judge will fill in the date of the judgment and sign it at the hearing.

Be sure to review the section in the previous chapter, concerning preparing the FINAL JUDGMENT AND DECREE after the hearing if the judge directs you to make changes.

You will also need to fill in a REPORT OF DIVORCE, ANNULMENT OR DISSOLUTION OF MARRIAGE. You will probably be given one of these by the clerk, but if not, use Form 24 in appendix C. Just fill in the information required for each box on the form.

NEGOTIATING AGREEMENTS 8

It is beyond the scope and ability of this book to fully present a course in negotiation techniques. However, a few basic rules may be of some help.

Ask for more than you want. This always gives you some room to compromise by giving up a few things, and ending up with close to what you really want. With property division, this means you will review your PROPERTY INVENTORY (Form 1), and decide which items you really want, would like to have, and don't care much about. Also try to figure out which items your spouse really wants, would like to have, and doesn't care much about. At the beginning you will say that you want certain things. Your list will include: (a) Everything you really want, (b) almost everything you'd like to have, (c) some of the things you don't care about, and (d) some of the things you think your spouse really wants or would like to have. Once you find out what is on your spouse's list, you begin trading items. Generally you try to give your spouse things that he or she really wants and that you don't care about, in return for your spouse giving you the items you really care about and would like to have.

Generally, child custody tends to be something that cannot be negotiated. It is more often used as a threat by one of the parties in order to get something else, such as more of the property, or lower child support.

If the real issue is one of these other matters, don't be concerned by a threat of a custody fight. In these cases the other party probably doesn't really want custody, and won't fight for it. If the real issue is custody, you won't be able to negotiate for it and will end up letting the judge decide anyway.

If you will be receiving child support you should first work out what you think the judge will order based upon the child support guidelines discussed in chapter 4. Then you should ask for more, and negotiate down to what the guidelines call for. If your spouse won't settle for something very close to the guidelines, give up trying to work it out and let the judge decide.

Let your spouse start the bidding. The first person to mention a dollar figure loses. Whether it's a child support figure or the value of a piece of property, try to get your spouse to name the amount he or she thinks it should be first. If your spouse starts with a figure almost what you had in mind, it will be much easier to get to your figure. If your spouse begins with a figure far from yours, you know how far in the other direction to begin your bid.

Give your spouse time to think and worry. Your spouse is probably just as afraid as you about the possibility of losing to the judge's decision, and would like to settle. Don't be afraid to state your "final offer," then walk away. Give your spouse a day or two to think it over. Maybe he or she will call back and make a better offer. If not, you can always "reconsider" and make a different offer in a few days, but don't be too willing to do this or your spouse may think you will give in even more.

Know your bottom line. Before you begin negotiating you should try to set a point that you will not go beyond. If you have decided that there are four items of property that you absolutely must have, and your spouse is only willing to agree to let you have three, it's time to end the bargaining session and go home.

Remember what you've learned. By the time you've read this far you should be aware of two things:

1. The judge will roughly divide your property equally.

2. The judge will probably follow the child support guidelines.

This awareness should give you an approximate idea of how things will turn out if the judge is asked to decide these issues, which should help you to set your bottom line on them.

The Court Hearing 9

Keep in mind that in Georgia, if your case is contested, the first hearing is a *temporary hearing*, and the judge's decision will be in the form of a *temporary order*. The temporary hearing is primarily concerned with child custody, child support, and who gets the marital residence. You are usually only allowed one witness at a temporary hearing. You may be entitled to submit affidavits. If affidavits are important to your case, I repeat that an attorney might be a good idea. In any event, if the judge's temporary decision in the temporary hearing is satisfactory, and the parties agree to all of the issues, then you will not need a final hearing. You may simply agree with your spouse to let the temporary order become final. If one of the parties wants to try for a better deal in the final, an attorney is going to just about be a necessity.

Preparation

SETTING A
HEARING DATE

One of the first things you will need to do is schedule a hearing date. See chapter 5 for instructions on setting a hearing date.

NOTIFYING
YOUR SPOUSE

Now that you've got a hearing date set with the judge, you'll need to notify your spouse of when the hearing will be. Even if you can easily call your spouse on the phone and notify him or her of the hearing, it is also proper to send a formal RULE NISI (notice of hearing) (Form 6).

Just fill in the RULE NISI form according to the instructions in chapter 5. Make three copies of the RULE NISI form, and mail one copy to your spouse. File the original with the court clerk, and keep two copies for yourself.

WHAT PAPERS
TO BRING

Bring your copies (if available) of the following papers to the hearing:

❏   Your PETITION FOR DIVORCE and the affidavits you attached to it.

❏   Any papers you may have showing that your spouse was properly notified of the divorce (although the Sheriff's affidavit of serving papers will be in the court file, and you may not have a copy).

❏   Any papers you may have to support what is in your DOMESTIC RELATIONS FINANCIAL AFFIDAVIT. This should include copies of your most recent paystub, Federal income tax return, and W-2 forms.

❏   Any paper's showing your spouse's income or property.

❏   Your settlement agreement, if you have one that hasn't yet been filed with the court.

❏   The FINAL JUDGMENT AND DECREE (Form 16) and CIVIL CASE DISPOSITION FORM (Form 10).

CIVIL CASE
DISPOSITION
FORM

To complete the CIVIL CASE DISPOSITION FORM (Form 10):

1.   Type in the name of the county where the court is located on the line before the word "COUNTY."

2.   Type in your name, address and phone number on the lines below the word "ATTORNEY(S)." Type "Pro Se" after your name.

3.   Type in the date of your final hearing after the words "DISPOSITION DATE."

4.   If you had an uncontested case, check the box for "Plaintiff" under the heading PRE-TRIAL DISPOSITIONS," and below

that check the box for "CONSENT JUDGMENT." If you had a contested case, and the judge decided matters, check "Plaintiff" under the heading "BENCH TRIAL," and check the box below that for "JUDGMENT FOR PLAINTIFF/DEFENDANT" and cross out the word "DEFENDANT."

THE HEARING

Your hearing will probably take place in a large courtroom like you see on TV or in the movies. It may also be in what looks more like a conference room. If so, the judge will be at the head of a table, with you and your spouse on either side.

The judge may start the hearing by summarizing what you are there for, then ask you and your spouse if you have any additional evidence to present, and then ask each of you any questions he may have. The judge will review the papers you filed with the clerk, and will probably ask you whether you understand and agree with what is in the papers. He will also ask you to explain why your marriage is "irretrievably broken." Just tell him why you're getting divorced. (Example 1: "We just don't have any interests in common anymore, and have drifted apart." Example 2: "My husband has had several affairs.")

If you have any information that is significantly different and more current than what is in the DOMESTIC RELATIONS FINANCIAL AFFIDAVITS, you should mention to the judge that you have more current information. You will then give a copy of whatever papers you have to show the changed situation (such as a current paystub showing an increase in pay, or a current bank statement showing a new balance).

The judge may ask to see any papers you have to prove what you've put in your DOMESTIC RELATIONS FINANCIAL AFFIDAVIT. Your basic job at the hearing is to answer the judge's questions, and to give the information needed for a divorce.

If there are any items that you and your spouse have not yet agreed upon, tell the judge what these items are. Refer to chapter 7, relating to the contested divorce, for more information about how to handle these unresolved issues. Be prepared to make a suggestion as to how these matters should be settled, and to explain to the judge why your suggestion is the best solution.

If the judge asks for any information that you haven't brought with you, tell the judge that you don't have it with you but you will be happy to provide him with the information by the end of the following day. Just be sure you get the papers to him!

At the end of the hearing the judge will tell you if he is going to grant you a divorce and accept your settlement agreement. It would be very unusual for him not to grant the divorce and accept your agreement. You will then tell the judge that you've prepared a proposed judgment, and hand him the original. Refer to chapters 6 and 7 regarding the FINAL JUDGMENT AND DECREE. You will need two extra copies of the FINAL JUDGMENT AND DECREE, one for yourself and one for your spouse. You should also bring two envelopes, one addressed to yourself and one addressed to your spouse, and two stamps. This is in case the judge wants to review the FINAL JUDGMENT AND DECREE and mail it to you later, instead of signing it at the hearing. If the judge wants you to make any changes in the FINAL JUDGMENT AND DECREE, make a careful note of exactly what the judge wants (ask him to explain it again if you didn't understand the first time), then tell the judge that you will make the correction and deliver the judgment the following day. If the change requested is a small one, you might even be able to write in the change by hand at the hearing.

If child support or alimony is to be paid, you will also need to bring a third copy of the FINAL JUDGMENT AND DECREE. Each county has a procedure for income deduction from employers (sometimes called *income deduction orders*) and these procedures are handled through the Child Support Recovery Office. If you wish your child support handled through the county office, call and ask for the appropriate forms.

When the hearing is over, thank the judge and leave. The judge will sign the original FINAL JUDGMENT AND DECREE, and send it to the court clerk's office to be entered in the court's file. Take the copies of the FINAL JUDGMENT AND DECREE and income deduction order (if appropriate) to the judge's secretary. The secretary will write in the date and use a stamp with the judge's name on each copy to authenticate them.

If any serious problems develop at the hearing (such as your spouse's attorney starts making a lot of technical objections, or the judge gives you a hard time), just tell the judge you'd like to continue the hearing so you can retain an attorney. Then go get one!

THE FUTURE

Once your divorce is final you are legally free to get married again. If you ever find yourself thinking about marriage, *be careful* before getting married again. Now that you know and appreciate how difficult it can be to get out of a marriage, you have no excuse for rushing into another one. If you do decide to get married, you would be wise to consider a premarital agreement. This is an agreement made before marriage, in which both parties disclose all of their property and debts, and agree how things will be handled in the event they separate. A premarital agreement can avoid a long and costly divorce. The book *How to Write Your Own Premarital Agreement* (including how you can convince your spouse-to-be that it is a good idea) can be obtained from your local bookstore or directly from the publisher.

In the past, the state governments helped collect child support through a law called the Uniform Reciprocal Enforcement of Support Act (abbreviated URESA). However, the system (as you may have heard) didn't work very well. The newest system is called the Uniform Interstate Family Support Act (UIFSA), and new rules are being written. Until the new law goes into effect, however, there are two agencies you need to be aware of:

CHILD SUPPORT
RECOVERY
OFFICE

The Child Support Recovery Office is the agency (called a *depository*) that processes the child support and alimony payments. This is frequently a division of the court clerk's office. The spouse responsible to pay the support (or his or her employer) will make payments to the depository. The depository then cashes that check and issues a check to the spouse entitled to receive support or alimony. Sometimes the judge's secretary or the court clerk will take an extra copy of the Final Judgment and send it to the central depository. The central depository keeps the official records of what has and has not been paid.

CHILD SUPPORT
ENFORCEMENT
OFFICE

The Child Support Enforcement Office is responsible for enforcing the payment of child support to custodial parents receiving welfare (Aid to Families with Dependent Children), and others who request their services. If you are to receive support and you would like to use the enforcement services of this office, you will need to contact your local Child Support Enforcement Office. This may not be necessary if your spouse goes on an income deduction order immediately, and keeps his or her job. But if some payments are missed, you may call the Child Support Enforcement office at any time and ask for their assistance.

INCOME
DEDUCTION
ORDER

You may also request payment of child support through an INCOME DEDUCTION ORDER (Form 26). The information to be filled in on each blank line is described immediately after each line. To make the process of obtaining an income deduction order easier, you may put a provision in the child support paragraph of your AGREEMENT that states: "The parent receiving support shall have the right to submit an income deduction order at his or her sole election." (You will note that such a provision is already contained in Form 13.) This may result in the court simply approving your INCOME DEDUCTION ORDER without the need for any further court hearings.

Send the INCOME DEDUCTION ORDER to the judge who signed your original divorce judgment, along with a copy of your agreement or order that gives you the right to request payment through income deduction (you may even want to highlight that provision). Even if that judge is no longer there, his or her replacement may sign the order and return it to you. Once you receive the signed order, send it to your spouse's employer by certified, return-receipt mail along with a NOTICE TO PAYOR (Form 27). You should soon begin receiving support payment directly from the employer.

NOTICE TO PAYOR

Along with the INCOME DEDUCTION ORDER, you will need to complete a NOTICE TO PAYOR (Form 27). This form gives the employer important information about the employer's rights and responsibilities connected with the INCOME DEDUCTION ORDER. As with the INCOME DEDUCTION ORDER, there is a notation after each blank line on the NOTICE TO PAYOR describing what information needs to be filled in on that line. The NOTICE TO PAYOR needs to be submitted to the judge for signature along with the INCOME DEDUCTION ORDER. Once signed by the judge and returned to you, it needs to be sent to the employer along with the INCOME DEDUCTION ORDER.

WHEN YOU CAN'T FIND YOUR SPOUSE 10

Your spouse has run off, and you have no idea of where he or she might be. So how do you have the sheriff deliver a copy of your PETITION FOR DIVORCE to your spouse? The answer is, you can't use the sheriff. Instead of personal service, you will use a method of giving notice called *service by publication*. This is one of the most complicated procedures in the legal system. You will need to follow the steps listed below very carefully.

THE DILIGENT SEARCH

The court will only permit publication when you can't locate your spouse. This also includes the situation where the sheriff has tried several times to personally serve your spouse, but it appears that your spouse is hiding to avoid being served. First, you'll have to show that you can't locate your spouse by letting the court know what you've done to try to find him or her. In making this search you should try the following:

- ☛ Check the phone book and directory assistance in the area where you live.

☛ Check directory assistance in the area where you last knew your spouse to be.

☛ Ask friends and relatives who might know where your spouse might be.

☛ Check with the post office where he or she last lived to see if there is a forwarding address. (You can ask by mail if it is too far away.)

☛ Check records of the tax collector and property assessor to see if your spouse owns property.

☛ Write to the Department of Motor Vehicles to see if your spouse has any car registrations.

☛ Check with any other sources you know that may lead you to a current address (such as landlords, prior employers, etc.).

If you do come up with a current address, go back to personal service by the sheriff, but if not, continue with this procedure.

PREPARING AND FILING COURT PAPERS

Once you have made your search you need to notify the court. This is done by filing the AFFIDAVIT OF PUBLICATION AND DILIGENT SEARCH (Form 19). This form tells the court what you've done to try to locate your spouse, and asks for permission to publish your notice. (If your spouse lives in another state, and you do have his or her address, this procedure may not be appropriate, and it is probably advisable to seek counsel. Georgia has a *long-arm statute* that the Court may require to be used in your circumstances. In any event, since this is fairly complicated, you may want to call the sheriff in the county and state where your spouse lives and arrange for personal service by the sheriff.)

To complete the AFFIDAVIT OF PUBLICATION AND DILIGENT SEARCH (Form 19) you need to:

1. Complete the top portion of the form according to the instructions in chapter 5.

2. Fill in the blanks with what you have done to find your spouse. Use more space if necessary.

3. Type in your name, address and phone number on the lines below the "Affiant Signature" line.

4. Sign your name on the "Affiant Signature" line, and fill in the date, before a notary public.

You can first try simply mailing the affidavit to the Clerk of Superior Court for filing, along with the blank ORDER OF PUBLICATION (Form 20) and a partially completed NOTICE OF PUBLICATION (Form 21). If that does not work, you will need to have a hearing. Some judges may let you file this action by a motion, and some will require a hearing. For safety's sake, you may want to seek counsel to determine the best process. To partially complete the NOTICE OF PUBLICATION (Form 21) you need to:

1. Complete the top portion according to the instructions in chapter 5.

2. Type in your spouse's name after the word "TO:"

3. Leave blank the spaces in the first and second lines of the main paragraph. On the fourth line, type in the word "Divorce."

4. In the sixth line, type in your address. The judge and clerk will complete the other parts of Form 21.

THE CLERK'S JOB

If the judge issues an order, then the clerk will fill in the remaining blanks on Form 21, and return two copies to you. If the clerk finds any errors in your papers, he will notify you about what needs to be corrected. You should provide the clerk with a self-addressed, stamped envelope when you deliver or send him these papers.

PUBLISHING

Your next step is to have a newspaper publish your NOTICE OF PUBLICATION (Form 21). Check the yellow pages listings under "Newspapers," and call several of the smaller ones in your county (making sure it is in the same county as the court), and ask if they are approved for legal announcements. If they are, ask how much they charge to publish a NOTICE OF PUBLICATION which does not involve property. What you are searching for is the cheapest paper. Some metropolitan Atlanta counties have a paper that specializes in the publishing of legal announcements, at a much cheaper rate than the regular daily newspapers. If you look around the courthouse you may be able to find a copy or newsstand for this paper.

Once you've found the paper you want, send them a copy of the NOTICE OF PUBLICATION (Form 21) and the ORDER OF PUBLICATION (Form 20), along with a short cover letter stating:

```
Enclosed is a Notice of Publication for publi-
cation as required by law.

Please take notice of the return date in the
Notice of Publication, and ensure that the date
of first publication is at least 60 days before
the return date. If you cannot comply with this
requirement, please notify me immediately so I
may obtain a revised Notice of Publication.
```

Be sure to include a check for the cost of publication, or to comply with whatever other payment arrangements you make with the paper.

The NOTICE OF PUBLICATION will be published once a week for four weeks. Get a copy of the paper the first time it will appear and check to be sure it was printed correctly. If you find an error, notify the newspaper immediately.

Also, look at the date the clerk put in the NOTICE OF PUBLICATION in the blank space after the words "Answer in writing within sixty (60) days of." You must make sure that this date is at least sixty days after the date the newspaper first published the NOTICE OF PUBLICATION. If this requirement is not met, notify the newspaper of their mistake. Remind them of your cover letter if necessary. You will also need to prepare a new ORDER OF PUBLICATION and NOTICE OF PUBLICATION for the clerk to sign, and then go through this procedure again. If the newspaper made the mistake, they should not charge you for the second publication.

As indicated in the NOTICE OF PUBLICATION, your spouse has until a certain date to respond. If your spouse responds to the notice published in the newspaper, proceed with either the uncontested or contested procedure as necessary. If your spouse does not respond by the date indicated in the NOTICE OF PUBLICATION, proceed with the uncontested divorce procedure as discussed in chapter 6.

SPECIAL CIRCUMSTANCES 11

WHEN YOU CAN'T AFFORD COURT COSTS

An AFFIDAVIT OF INDIGENCE (Form 22), is for use when you cannot afford to pay the filing fee and other costs associated with the divorce. In order to qualify for a waiver of the filing fee, you must be *indigent*. If you are indigent, your income is probably low enough for you to qualify for public assistance (i.e., welfare).

Caution: If you decide to use this form, you will probably be asked for more information to prove that you meet the requirements for being declared indigent, and therefore, eligible to have the filing and service fees waived. Before you file this form, you may want to see if the court clerk will give you any information on what is required to be declared indigent. You should also be aware that you can be held in contempt of court for giving false information on this form.

To complete the AFFIDAVIT OF INDIGENCE (Form 22):

1. Complete the top portion according to the instructions in chapter 5.

2. Do not sign this form yet. But do type in your name, address and phone number where indicated under the line marked "Affiant."

3. Take this form to a notary, and sign it before the notary on the line marked "Affiant." The notary will then date and sign the form. This form is now ready for filing.

PROTECTING YOURSELF, YOUR CHILDREN, AND YOUR PROPERTY

Some people have two special concerns when getting prepared to file for a divorce: Fear of physical attack by their spouse, and fear that their spouse will try to take the marital property and hide it. There are additional legal papers you can file if you feel you are in either of these situations.

PROTECTING YOURSELF

Most counties have a procedure through which a PETITION FOR FAMILY VIOLENCE PROTECTION (Form 28) may be filed. The court will probably have its own petition form for you to use, but fill out Form 28 and take it with you to the court. Form 28 will have most, if not all, of the information you will need to fill out the court's form. Filling out this document is similar to completing the PETITION FOR DIVORCE (Form 11). The form itself indicates what information is to be inserted in each blank space. In paragraph 3, be specific—and don't lie! It is extremely important to tell the truth. If your spouse threatened to hit you, write down that you were threatened and were scared, but don't say you were actually hit if you were not. This is a very serious matter, and your credibility is at issue.

If the judge agrees that your situation is a family issue, and that violence is likely to occur or has occurred, he or she may issue immediate restraining orders taking the offending party out of the house and away from you or the children. This only lasts a few days, however, and a hearing will be held within a very short period of time to see if the problem has been resolved, or whether the offending party should stay separated from the family. The judge can also award the victim temporary living expenses, child support, and custody. The new domestic violence statutes are very powerful, but judges have different interpretations of their legal authority and the application of the statutes can be uneven. In some cases, violent husbands have been hauled out of their home with nothing but the clothes on their back and a set of car keys (and if there is only one car, the offender often must call a cab)!

Be sure to file your petition in the county where your spouse is living (or where he or she has gone), otherwise the court can't enforce the order.

Most domestic attorneys, battered spouse agencies, family service facilities, and legal aid societies are also equipped to promptly assist you in preparing the necessary documents. Attorneys can also assist you with more elaborate procedures such as temporary protective orders. This process is similar to a family violence petition, but many courts handle these differently.

PROTECTING YOUR CHILDREN

Protecting your children from abuse can be handled in the PETITION FOR FAMILY VIOLENCE PROTECTION (Form 28). If you are worried that your spouse may try to kidnap your children, you should make sure that the day care center, baby-sitter, relative, or whomever you leave the children with at any time, is aware that you are in the process of a divorce and that the children are only to be released to you personally (not to your spouse or to any other relative, friend, etc.). To prevent your spouse from taking the children out of the United States, you can apply for a passport for each child. Once a passport is issued, the government will not issue another. So get their passport and lock it up in a safe deposit box. (This won't prevent them from being taken to Canada or Mexico, where passports are not required, but will prevent them from being taken overseas). You can also file a motion to prevent the removal of the children from the state and to deny passport services. Forms for this motion are discussed in at the beginning of appendix C, in the section titled "Where to Find Additional Forms."

PROTECTING YOUR PROPERTY

If you genuinely fear that your spouse will try to remove money from bank accounts and try to hide important papers showing what property you own, you may want to take this same action before your spouse can. However, you can make a great deal of trouble for yourself with the judge if you do this to try to get these assets for yourself. So, make a complete list of any property you do take, and be sure to include these items in your DOMESTIC RELATIONS FINANCIAL AFFIDAVIT (Form 12). You may need to convince the judge that you only took these items temporarily, in order to preserve them until a FINAL JUDGMENT AND DECREE is entered. Also, do not spend any cash you take from a bank account, or sell or give away any items of property you take. Any cash should be placed in a separate bank account, without your spouse's name on it, and kept separate from any other cash you have. Any papers, such as deeds, car titles, stock or bond certificates, etc., should be placed in a safe deposit box, without your spouse's name on it. The idea is not to take these things for yourself, but to get them in a safe place so your spouse can't hide them and deny they ever existed.

If your spouse is determined and resourceful, there is no guaranteed way to prevent the things discussed in this section from happening. All you can do is put as many obstacles in his or her way as possible, so he or she may suffer legal consequences for acting improperly.

TEMPORARY SUPPORT AND CUSTODY

If your spouse has left you with the children, the mortgage, and monthly bills, and is not helping you financially, you need to ask the clerk to be sure that a RULE NISI (Form 6), and the "Standing Order of the Court" (a form available in all Superior Court Clerk's offices) are served along with the PETITION FOR DIVORCE. The RULE NISI will give you a temporary hearing date, at which you may ask the court to order the payment of support for you and the children during the divorce procedure. Of course, if you were the only person bringing in income and have been paying all the bills, it is difficult to be awarded much support. There are also criminal charges that can be brought if the breadwinner leaves the family without support for at least thirty days.

TAXES

As you are no doubt aware, the United States' income tax code is complicated and ever-changing. For this reason it is impossible to give detailed information with respect to taxes in a book such as this. Any such information could easily be out of date by the time of publication. Therefore, it is strongly recommended that you consult your accountant, lawyer, or whomever prepares your tax return about the tax consequences of a divorce. A few general concerns are discussed in this chapter, to give you an idea of some of the tax questions that can arise.

PROPERTY DIVISION AND TAXES

You and your spouse may be exchanging title to property as a result of your divorce. Generally, there will not be any tax to pay as the result of such a transfer. However, whomever gets a piece of property will be responsible to pay any tax that may become due upon sale. This amount may be substantial in regard to transfers of property or investments.

The Internal Revenue Service (I.R.S.) has issued numerous rulings about how property is to be treated in divorce situations. You need to be especially careful if you are transferring any tax shelters, or other complicated financial arrangements.

Be sure to read the following section on alimony, because fancy property settlements are asking for tax problems.

ALIMONY AND TAXES

Alimony can cause the most tax problems of any aspect of divorce. The I.R.S. is always making new rulings on whether an agreement is really alimony, or is really property division. The basic rule is that alimony is treated as income to the person receiving it, and as a deduction for the person paying it. Therefore, in order to manipulate the tax consequences, many couples try to show something as part of the property settlement, instead of as alimony; or the reverse. As the I.R.S. becomes aware of these tax "games" it issues rulings on how it will view a certain arrangement. If you are simply talking about the regular, periodic payment of cash, the I.R.S. will probably not question that it is alimony. But if you try to call it property settlement, you may run into problems. The important thing is to consult a tax expert if you are considering any unusual or creative property settlement or alimony arrangements.

CHILD SUPPORT
AND TAXES

There are simple tax rules regarding child support:

1. Whoever has custody gets to claim the children on his or her tax return, both for a deduction and for the new $500 credit (unless both parents file a special I.R.S. form agreeing to a different arrangement each year).

2. The parent receiving child support does not need to report it as income.

3. The parent paying child support cannot deduct it.

If you are sharing physical custody, the parent with whom the child lives for the most time during the year is entitled to claim the child as a dependent.

The I.R.S. form to reverse this must be filed each year. Therefore, if you and your spouse have agreed that you will get to claim the children (even though you don't have custody), you should have your spouse to sign an open-ended form that you can file each year, so that you don't have to worry about it each year. A phone call to the I.R.S. can help you get answers to questions on this point.

PENSION PLANS

Pension plans, or retirement plans, of you and your spouse are marital assets. They may be very valuable assets. If you and your spouse are young, and have not been working very long, you may not have pension plans worth worrying about. Also, if you have both worked, and have similar pensions plans, it may be best just to include a provision in your settlement agreement that "each party shall keep his or her own pension plan." But if you have been married a long time, and your spouse worked while you stayed home to raise the children, your spouse's pension plan may be worth a lot of money, and may be necessary to see you through retirement. If you and your spouse cannot agree on how to divide a pension plan, you should see an attorney. The valuation of pension plans, and how they are to be divided, is a complicated matter that you should not attempt.

Be sure to include all three types of pension accounts in your negotiations (if you have all three). IRAs are fairly simple, but defined contribution plans [401(k)s and Keoghs] and defined benefit plans (retirement accounts) are extremely complicated matters. Expect to pay $500 and up for a CPA or lawyer to determine the division of these.

MILITARY DIVORCES

This can be a topic for an entire book, but a military divorce has separate issues to resolve. First, it is often unclear where the divorce needs to be filed. Second, the Federal Government has established procedures that are addressed in dividing miliary pensions. Finally, even beginning a divorce proceeding against a service member may trigger the *Soldiers' and Sailors' Civil Relief Act.*

SOLDIERS' AND SAILORS' CIVIL RELIEF ACT

Congress recognized that military service places service members at a disadvantage in some situations. For example, it can be difficult for a service member to defend a lawsuit if his military duties prevent him from appearing in court. For this reason, Congress enacted the Soldiers' and Sailors' Civil Relief Act of 1940. This law provides certain protections to persons who are on active duty in the armed forces. The purpose of this Act is to enable service members to devote themselves to the defense of the country, by relieving them of the fear that someone will take advantage of them during their period of service. However, the statute does not permit a service member to avoid his or her legal obligations, nor does it discharge or relieve those obligations.

The Soldiers' and Sailors' Civil Relief Act provides for the temporary suspension of civil (*not* criminal) legal proceedings when a service member's ability to prosecute or defend that action is adversely affected by military duties. For example, if you are sued in another state and cannot get leave to attend the trial, you should be able to get the case delayed until you can get leave. On the other hand, civil proceedings will normally not be delayed when military duties have no impact—thus, if the only reason you cannot attend court is that you cannot afford the plane fare, a delay is unlikely to be granted. (However, the Act also provides for the appointment of an attorney to protect the service member's interests when the member cannot appear.)

The Soldiers' and Sailors' Civil Relief Act also provides the following rights to service members: (1) protection from foreclosure and repossession on debts incurred prior to military service; (2) reduction of interest rates to six percent on debts incurred prior to military service; (3) right to terminate a lease made prior to military service; (4) protection of dependents from eviction, under very limited circumstances; (5) payment of life insurance premiums by the government, when the service member is unable to do so; (6) relief from taxation by a state where a service member is stationed pursuant to military orders; and (7) protection from default judgments. When a service member's military duties affect his or her ability to either prosecute or defend a lawsuit, the Soldiers' and Sailors' Civil Relief Act provides some relief.

In divorce, child custody, and paternity cases, the courts are extremely reluctant to issue a lengthy stay or set aside a judgment, but assistance in this area is regularly provided by the military lawyers on base.

MILITARY PERSONNEL STATIONED IN GEORGIA

Generally, if the soldier has been stationed in Georgia for at least one year, you can file in any county which borders the military base to which he or she is assigned. If they have been transferred out of the country, it is the county bordering the military base to which they were last assigned. Remember however, that in Georgia, parties can generally agree to a county to file in if one of them has lived there for more than six months preceding the filing of the divorce.

PATERNITY AND NAME CHANGES

PATERNITY

Paternity can be established voluntarily through a *paternity affidavit* in which the natural father admits paternity. If the alleged father disputes paternity, there are two tests available to him: (1) the traditional blood testing, and (2) "DNA fingerprinting," which compares the genetic material of father, mother, and child. While neither test can conclusively establish paternity, they will be given considerable weight by the court and will probably suffice to establish paternity in the absence of compelling evidence to the contrary. Both tests are capable of conclusively disproving paternity. The Child Support Enforcement Agency can set up a blood test if the father is willing to take one.

NAME CHANGE FOR WIFE

Name changes in Georgia are done through the courts. When taken in conjunction with a divorce, the wife can ask to have her maiden name restored at no additional charge. This free service does not apply to changing the name of minor children. If a name change is likely, this is the appropriate time to take advantage of the opportunity, because it can cost several hundred dollars to legally change your name outside of the divorce process.

NAME CHANGE FOR CHILDREN

Georgia also has a law providing that the name of the child can be changed if the father has no contact with the child and is not paying support. Ask a local attorney for the particulars, since this can be tricky.

ADOPTION

An adoption confers upon the adoptive parent all of the rights and obligations of the natural parent, and terminates the rights and obligations of the affected natural parent. Thus, the natural parent no longer is under an obligation to support, but also loses visitation rights, and the child is no longer his/her natural heir. (A step-parent has no legal right to name a guardian for a child, which can be inconvenient if the custodial natural parent dies; a step-parent adoption can avoid this difficulty.)

Because of its significant consequences, the consent of the natural parent(s) whose rights are being terminated is usually required. The adoption of foreign nationals can be a particularly complicated matter, not only because of the problems related to the adoption but also because of immigration issues.

The complexities of the adoption process almost require the assistance of an attorney, but it is possible for the process to cost as little as $500.

GRANDPARENT VISITATION OR CUSTODY

Under Georgia law, it is very difficult for grandparents to be awarded visitation, even when it is in the best interests of the child. It is also possible for grandparents (and other third parties) to get custody of the children when it is in their best interest. This area of the law is changing daily, though. So if this applies to you, talk to an attorney about the rules that are currently in effect. Also, see the book *Grandparents' Rights*, by Traci Truly, also published by Sourcebooks, Inc., which is available through your local bookstore or directly from the publisher.

Appendix A
Superior Court Clerks

Appling County
F. Floyd Hunter
Courthouse Square
Baxley, GA 31513
912-367-8126

Atkinson County
W.M. Smith
P.O. Box 6
Pearson, GA 31642
912-422-3343

Bacon County
Rena Hutto
P.O. Box 376
Alma, GA 31510
912-632-4915

Baker County
Betty Bush
P.O. Box 10
Newton, GA 31770
912-734-3004

Baldwin County
Rosemary Ivey Fordham
P.O. Drawer 987
Milledgeville, GA 31061
912-453-6324

Banks County
Clifton B. Hill
P.O. Box 337
Homer, GA 30547
404-677-2320

Barrow County
Syble H. Brock
P.O. Box 1280
Winder, GA 30680
404-307-3035

Bartow County
Grady Jefferson
P.O. Box 749
Cartersville, GA 30120
912-382-2930

Ben Hill County
Audrey D. Jordan
P.O. Box 1104
Fitzgerald, GA 31850
912-423-3736

Berrien County
Bonnie Moore Murphy
Berrien County
Courthouse
Nashville, GA 31639
912-686-5506

Bibb County
Aline T. Byrd
P.O. Box 1015
Macon, GA 31202
912-749-6527

Bleckley County
Dianne C. Brown
Bleckley County
Courthouse
306 SE Second St.
Cochran, GA 31014
912-934-3210

Brantley County
M. Anthony Ham
P.O. Box 1067
Nahunta, GA 31553
912-462-5635

Brooks County
Elizabeth D. Baker
P.O. Box 630
Quitman, GA 31643
912-263-4747

Bryan County
Sherra B. Chassereau
P.O. Drawer H
Pembroke, GA 31321
912-653-4681

Bulloch County
Sherri A. Atkins
Bulloch County
Courthouse
Statesboro, GA 30458
912-764-9009

Burke County
Torbit Banks, Jr.
P.O. Box 803
Waynesboro, GA
30830
404-554-2279

Butts County
David P. Ridgeway
P.O. Box 320
Jackson, GA 30233
404-775-8215

Calhoun County
James C. Shippey
P.O. Box 68
Morgan, GA 31766
912-849-2715

Camden County
Carolyn A. Warren
P.O. Box 578
Woodbine, GA 31569
912-576-5601, Ext. 210

Candler County
Theresa K. Gray
P.O. Box 830
Metter, GA 30439
912-685-5257

Carroll County
Kenneth H. Skinner
P.O. Box 1620
Carrollton, GA 30117
404-834-0064

Catoosa County
Norman L. Stone
Catoosa County
    Courthouse
Ringgold, GA 30736

Charlton County
Inez B. Southwell
Charlton County
    Courthouse
Folkston, GA 31537
912-496-2354

Chatham County
Doris S. Stephens
304 Chatham County
    Courthouse
133 Montgomery St.
Savannah, GA 31499
912-652-7200

Chattahoochee County
Louis Maxwell
P.O. Box 120
Cusseta, GA 31805
404-989-3424

Chattooga County
Sam L. Cordle, Jr.
P.O. Box 159
Summerville, GA 30747
404-857-2594

Cherokee County
Annette Fleming
100 North St., Room 3
Canton, GA 30114
404-479-0538

Clarke County
Dolores Brooks
P.O. Box 1805
Athens, GA 30603
404-354-2781

Clay County
Deanna Bertrand
P.O. Box 550
Fort Gaines, GA 31751
912-768-2631

Clayton County
Joe B. Mundy
202 Clayton County
    Courthouse
Jonesboro, GA 30236
404-477-3395

Clinch County
Daniel V. Leccese
P.O. Box 433
Homerville, GA 31634
912-487-2548

Cobb County
Jay C. Stephenson
30 Waddell St.
Marietta, GA 30090
404-528-1300

Coffee County
Willifred M. Thompson
Coffee County
    Courthouse
P.O. Box 886
Moultrie, GA 31776
912-384-2865

Colquitt County
Shirley T. Asbell
P.O. Box 886
Moultrie, GA 31776
912-985-1324

Columbia County
Mary W. Reeves
P.O. Box 100
Appling, GA 30802
404-556-6053

Cook County
Everett B. James
Cook County
    Courthouse
212 N. Hutchinson Ave.
Adel, GA 31620
912-896-7717

Cowetta County
Deborah P. Glover
P.O. Box 943
Newman, GA 30264
404-254-2690

Crawford County
John D. Castleberry
P.O. Box 419
Knoxville, GA 31050
912-836-3328

Crisp County
Ovis Stephens
P.O. Box 747
Cordele, GA 31015
912-276-2616

Dade County
Sarah D. Moore
P.O. Box 417
Trenton, GA 30752
404-657-4778

Dawson County
Curtis L. Chappell
P.O. Box 222
Dawsonville, GA 30534
404-265-2525

Decatur County
Zadie B. King
P.O. Box 336
Bainbridge, GA 31717
912-248-3025

Dekalb County
Carol Jones
Room 207
556 N. McDonough St.
Decatur, GA 30030
404-371-2762

Dodge County
Tommy Cranford
P.O. Drawer 4276
Eastman, GA 31023
912-374-2871

Dougherty County
Imanell Gable
P.O. Box 1827
Albany, GA 31703
912-431-2198

Douglas County
Jane C. Williams
Douglas County
    Courthouse
6754 Broad St.
Douglasville, GA 30134
404-949-2000, Ext. 256

Early County
Norman C. Alexander
P.O. Box 525
Blakely, GA 31723
912-723-3033

Echols County
Lola Davis
P.O. Box 213
Statenville, GA 31648
912-559-5642

Effingham County
Elizabeth Z. Hursey
P.O. Box 387
Springfield, GA 31329
912-754-6071, Ext. 118

Elbert County
Pat V. Anderson
P.O. Box 619
Elberton, GA 30635
404-283-2005

Emanuel County
Jay Lawson
P.O. Box 627
Swainsboro, GA 30401
912-237-8911

Evans County
Gail B. McCooey
P.O. Box 845
Claxton, GA 30417
912-739-3868

Fannin County
John W. Chastain
P.O. Box 1300
Blue Ridge, GA 30513
404-632-2039

Fayette County
W.A. Ballard
P.O. Box 130
Fayetteville, GA 30214
404-461-4703

Floyd County
Joe E. Johnston
P.O. Box 1110
Rome, GA 30163
404-291-5190

Forsyth County
Cecil McClure
Room 110
Forsyth County
    Courthouse
Cumming, GA 30130
404-781-2120

Franklin County
James A. LeCroy
P.O. Box 70
Carnesville, GA 30521
404-384-2514

Fulton County
Juanita Hicks
106 Fulton County
    Courthouse
136 Pryor St. SW
Atlanta, GA 30303
404-730-5300

Gilmer County
Willard Ralson
Gilmer County
Courthouse
#1 Westside Square
Ellijay, GA 30540
404-635-4462

Glascock County
Audrey H. Richards
P.O. Box 231
Gibson, GA 30810
404-598-2084

Glynn County
Michael E. Harrison, Sr.
P.O. Box 1355
Brunswick, GA 31521
912-267-5610

Gordon County
Lewis Couch
P.O. Box 367
Calhoun, GA 30703
404-629-9533

Grady County
Annette H. Alred
Box 8
250 North Broad St.
Cairo, GA 31728
912-377-2792

Greene County
Ray A. Marchman
Greene County
    Courthouse
Greensboro, GA 30642
404-453-3340

Gwinnett County
Gary R. Yates
P.O. Box 880
Lawrenceville, GA 30246
404-822-8100

Habersham County
Ernest W. Nations, Jr.
P.O. 108
Clarkesville, GA 30523
404-754-2923

Hall County
Dwight S. Wood
P.O. Box 1275
Gainesville, GA 30504
404-531-7037

Hancock County
Leroy S. Wiley
P.O. Box 451
Sparta, GA 31087
404-444-6444

Haralson County
Mary Ann Weatherby
P.O. Box 373
Buchanan, GA 30113
404-646-2005

Harris County
Rebecca B. Wynn
P.O. Box 528
Hamilton, GA 31811
404-628-4944

Hart County
William E. Holland, III
P.O. Box 386
Hartwell, GA 30643
404-376-7189

Heard County
Bryan Owensby
P.O. Box 249
Franklin, GA 30217
404-954-2121

Houston County
Carolyn V. Sullivan
Houston County
    Courthouse
800 Carroll St.
Perry, GA 31069
912-987-2170

Irwin County
Melba W. Paulk
P.O. Box 186
Ocilla, GA 31774
912-468-5356

Jackson County
Reba P. Parks
P.O. Box 7
Jefferson, GA 30549
404-367-1199, Ext. 250

Jasper County
Dan Jordan
Jasper County
    Courthouse
Monticello, GA 31064
404-468-6651

Jeff Davis County
Eula Mae Edwards
P.O. Box 248
Hazelhurst, GA 31539
912-375-6615

Jefferson County
Michael R. Jones
P.O. Box 151
Louisville, GA 30434
912-625-7922

Jenkins County
Nell O. Frye
P.O. Box 659
Millen, GA 30442
912-982-4683

Johnson County
Daley C. Powell
P.O. Box 321
Wrightsville, GA 31096
912-864-3484

Jones County
Bart W. Jackson
P.O. Box 39
Gray, GA 31032
912-986-6671

Lamar County
Robert F. Abbott
Lamar County
    Courthouse
326 Thomaston St.
Barnesville, GA 30204
404-358-2671

Lanier County
Martha B. Neugent
Lanier County
    Courthouse
Lakeland, GA 31635
912-482-3594

Laurens County
Roy Allen Thomas
P.O. Box 2028
Dublin, GA 31040
912-272-3210

Lee County
Martha D. Phillips
P.O. Box 2028
Leesburg, GA 31763
912-759-6018

Liberty County
F. Barry Wilkes
P.O. Box 50
Hinesville, GA 31313
912-876-3625

Lincoln County
Bruce C. Beggs
P.O. Box 340
Lincolnton, GA 30817
404-359-4444

Long County
Harrell Manning
P.O. Box 458
Ludowici, GA 31316
912-545-2123

Lowndes County
Sara L. Crow
P.O. Box 1349
Valdosta, GA 31601
912-333-5127

Lumpkin County
Edward E. Tucker
279 Courthouse Hill
Dahlonega, GA 30533
404-864-3736

Macon County
Sylvia H. Hogg
P.O. Box 337
Ogelthorpe, GA 31068

Madison County
Michelle H. Strickland
P.O. Box 247
Danielsville, GA 30633
404-795-3351

Marion County
Mary Jo Page
P.O. Box 41
Buena Vista, GA 31803
912-649-7321

McDuffie County
Constance H. Cheatham
P.O. Box 158
Thomson, GA 30824
404-595-2134

McIntosh County
Ann W. Poppell
P.O. Box 1661
Darien, GA 31305
912-437-6641

Meriwether County
Louise T. Garrett
P.O. Box 160
Meriwether County
    Courthouse
Greenville, GA 30222
404-672-4416

Miller County
Annie L. Middleton
P.O. Box 66
Colquitt, GA 31737
912-758-4102

Mitchell County
Dot B. Brown
P.O. Box 427
Camilla, GA 31730

Monroe County
Geraldine G. Ham
P.O. Box 450
Forsyth, GA 31029
912-994-7022

Montgomery County
Dwight Newsome
P.O. Box 311
Mount Vernon, GA 30445
912-583-4401

Morgan County
Elaine M. Mealor
P.O. Box 130
Madison, GA 30650
404-342-3605

Murray County
Loreine P. Mathews
P.O. Box 1000
Chatsworth, GA 30705
404-695-2932

Muscogee County
Linda Pierce
Newton County
    Courthouse
1124 Clark St.
Covington, GA 30209
404-784-2035

Oconee County
Sandra Glass
P.O. 113
Watkinsville, GA 30677
404-769-3940

Oglethorpe County
Beneva G. Stamey
P.O. Box 68
Lexington, GA 30648
404-743-5731

Paulding County
Sylvia G. Strickland
Room G-2, 11
Courthouse Square
Paulding County
    Courthouse
Dallas, GA 30132
404-445-8874

Peach County
Joe Wilder
P.O. Box 389
Fort Valley, GA 31030
912-825-5331

Pickens County
Mildred B. Mullinax
211 North Main St.
Jasper, GA 30143
404-692-2014

Pierce County
Martha G. Dixon
P.O. Box 588
Blackshear, GA 31516
912-449-2020

Pike County
L. Carolyn Williams
P.O. Box 10
Zebulon, GA 30295
404-567-8401

Polk County
Sandra W. Galloway
P.O. Box 948
Cedartown, GA 30125
404-749-2114

Pulaski County
Woodson Daniel
P.O. Box 88
Hawksville, GA 31036
912-783-1911

Putnam County
Elizabeth W. Cardwell
100 S. Jefferson St.
Putnam County
    Courthouse
Eatonton, GA 31024
404-485-4501

Quitman County
Peggy J. Sparks
P.O. Box 307
Georgetown, GA 31754
912-334-2578

Rabun County
Joe Jarrard
P.O. Box 893
Clayton, GA 30525
404-782-3615

Randolph County
Wynelle P. Wood
P.O. Box 98
Cuthbert, GA 31740
912-732-2216

Richmond County
J. Lester Newsome
P.O. Box 2046
Augusta, GA 30903
404-821-2443

Rockdale County
Joanne P. Caldwell
P.O. Box 937
Conyers, GA 30207
404-929-4021

Schley County
Ginger G. Eubanks
P.O. Box 7
Ellaville, GA 31806
912-937-5581

Screven County
Edith B. Pullen
P.O. Box 156
Sylvannia, GA 30467
912-564-2614

Seminole County
Sylivia G. James
P.O. Box 672
Donalsonville, GA 31745
912-524-2525

Spalding County
Myrtle F. Peebles
P.O. Box 163
Griffin, GA 30224
404-228-9900

Stephens County
Aubre Grafton
Stephens County
    Courthouse
Toccoa, GA 30577
404-886-3598

Stewart County
(Mrs.) Jerry E. Kelly
P.O. Box 910
Lumpkin, GA 31815
912-838-6220

Sumter County
Betty S. Shattles
P.O. Box 333
Americus, GA 31709
912-924-5626

Talbot County
Bonnell E. Parker
P.O. Box 325
Talbotton, GA 31827
404-665-3239

Taliaferro County
Mary R. Darden
P.O. Box 182
Crawfordville, GA 30631
404-456-2123

Tatnall County
Billie K. Rawls
P.O. Box 56
Reidsville, GA 30453
912-557-6716

Taylor County
Joye M. Parker
P.O. Box 248
Butler, GA 31006
912-862-5594

Telfair County
Betty Johnson
Telfair County
    Courthouse
McRae, GA 31055
912-868-6525

Terrell County
Louise Darley
P.O. Box 189
Dawson, GA 31742
912-995-2631

Thomas County
David Hutchings, Jr.
Thomasville, GA 31799
912-225-4108

Tift County
John T. Lindsey
P.O. Box 354
Tifton, GA 31793
912-386-7810

Toombs County
Chess Fountain
P.O. Box 530
Lyons, GA 30436
912-526-3501

Towns County
Cecil Ray Dye
P.O. Box 178
Hiawassee, GA 30546
404-896-2130

Treutlen County
Curtis Rogers, Jr.
P.O. Box 356
Sooperton, GA 30457
912-529-4215

Troup County
Ramona S. Ward
P.O. Box 866
LaGrange, GA 30241
404-883-1740

Turner County
Mamie Odom
P.O. Box 106
Ashburn, GA 31714
912-567-2011

Twiggs County
Pattie H. Grimsley
P.O. Box 228
Jeffersonville, GA 31044
912-945-3350

Union County
Allen Conley
114 Courthouse St.,
Box 5
Blairsville, GA 30512

Upson County
Nancy Adams
P.O. Box 469
Thomaston, GA 30286
404-647-7835

Walker County
Bill McDaniel
P.O. Box 448
LaFayette, GA 30728
404-638-1742

Walton County
Kathy K. Keese
P.O. Box 745
Monroe, GA 30655
404-267-1305

Ware County
Betty B. Kennedy
P.O. Box 776
Waycross, GA 31501
912-287-4340

Warren County
Martha Poole
P.O. Box 346
Warrenton, GA 30828
404-465-2262

Washington County
Janie L. Bryan
P.O. Box 231
Sandersville, GA 31082
912-522-3186

Wayne County
Stetson Bennett, Jr.
P.O. Box 918
Jessup, GA 31545
912-427-5930

Webster County
Tina Blankenship
P.O. Box 117
Preston, GA 31824
912-828-3525

Wheeler County
Michael Morrison
P.O. Box 38
Alamo, GA 30411
912-568-7137

White County
Carol Jackson
1650 S. Main St., Ste. B
Cleveland, GA 30528
404-865-2613

Whitfield County
Betty Nelson
P.O. Box 868
Dalton, GA 30720
404-275-7450

Wilcox County
James W. Hawkins
Wilcox County
    Courthouse
Abbeville, GA 31001
912-467-2442

Wilkes County
Jean F. Payne
Room 205
Wilkes County
    Courthouse
23 E. Court St.
Washington, GA
30673
404-678-2423

Wilkinson County
Cinda S. Bright
P.O. Box 250
Irwinton, GA 31042
912-946-2221

Worth County
Vera Kilcrease
Room 13
201 North Main St.
Sylvester, GA 31791
912-776-8205

APPENDIX B
GEORGIA CODE DIVORCE PROVISIONS

19-3-9. Each spouse's property separate.

The separate property of each spouse shall remain the separate property of that spouse, except as provided in Chapters 5 and 6 of this title and except as otherwise provided by law.

19-6-1. Alimony defined; when authorized; how determined; lien on estate of party dying prior to order; certain changes in parties' assets prohibited pending determination.

(a) Alimony is an allowance out of one party's estate, made for the support of the other party when living separately. It is either temporary or permanent.

(b) A party shall not be entitled to alimony if it is established by a preponderance of the evidence that the separation between the parties was caused by that party's adultery or desertion. In all cases in which alimony is sought, the court shall receive evidence of the factual cause of the separation even though one or both of the parties may also seek a divorce, regardless of the grounds upon which a divorce is sought or granted by the court.

(c) In all other cases in which alimony is sought, alimony is authorized, but is not required, to be awarded to either party in accordance with the needs of the party and the ability of the other party to pay. In determining whether or not to grant alimony, the court shall consider evidence of the conduct of each party toward the other.

(d) Should either party die prior to the court's order on the issue of alimony, any rights of the other party to alimony shall survive and be a lien upon the estate of the deceased party.

(e) Pending final determination by the court of the right of either party to alimony, neither party shall make any substantial change in the assets of the party's estate except in the course of ordinary business affairs and except for bona fide transfers for value.

19-6-4. When permanent alimony authorized; how enforced.

(a) Permanent alimony may be granted in the following cases:
  (1) In cases of divorce;
  (2) In cases of voluntary separation; or
  (3) Where one spouse, against the will of that spouse, is abandoned or driven off by the other spouse.

(b) A grant of permanent alimony may be enforced either by writ of fieri facias or by attachment for contempt.

19-6-5. Factors in determining amount of alimony; effect of remarriage on obligations for alimony.

(a) The finder of fact may grant permanent alimony to either party, either from the corpus of the estate or otherwise. The following shall be considered in determining the amount of alimony, if any, to be awarded:

(1) The standard of living established during the marriage;

(2) The duration of the marriage;

(3) The age and the physical and emotional condition of both parties;

(4) The financial resources of each party;

(5) Where applicable, the time necessary for either party to acquire sufficient education or training to enable him to find appropriate employment;

(6) The contribution of each party to the marriage, including, but not limited to, services rendered in homemaking, child care, education, and career building of the other party.

(7) The condition of the parties, including the separate estate, earning capacity, and fixed liabilities of the parties; and

(8) Such other relevant factors as the court deems equitable and proper.

(b) All obligations for permanent alimony, however created, the time for performance of which has not arrived, shall terminate upon the remarriage of the party to whom the obligations are owed unless otherwise provided.

19-6-15. Child support in final verdict or decree; computation of award; guidelines for determining amount of award; continuation of duty to provide support; duration of support.

(a) In the final verdict or decree, the trier of fact shall specify in what amount and from which party the minor children are entitled to permanent support. The final verdict or decree shall further specify in what manner, how often, to whom, and until when the support shall be paid. When support is awarded, the party who is required to pay the support shall not be liable to third persons for necessaries furnished to the children embraced in the verdict or decree. In any case in which child support is determined by a jury, the court shall charge the provisions of this Code section by the jury shall not be required to return a special interrogatory. Furthermore, nothing contained within this Code section shall prevent the parties from entering into an enforceable agreement to the contrary which may be made the order of the court pursuant to the review by the court of child support amounts contained in the Code section.

(b) The child support award shall be computed as provided in this subsection:

(1) Computation of child support shall be based upon gross income;

(2) For the purpose of determining the obligor's child support obligation, gross income shall include 100 percent of wage and salary income and other compensation for personal services, interest, dividends, net rental income, self-employment income, and all other income, except need-based public assistance;

(3) The earning capacity of an asset of a party available for child support may be used in determining gross income. The reasonable earning potential of an asset may be determined by multiplying its equity by a reasonable rate of interest. The amount generated by that calculation should be added to the obligor's gross income;

(4) Allowable expenses deducted to calculate self-employment income that personally benefit the obligor, or economic in-kind benefits received by an employed obligor, may be included in calculating the obligor's gross monthly income; and

(5) The amount of the obligor's child support obligation shall be determined by multiplying the obligor's gross income per pay period by a percentage based on the number of children for whom child support is being determined. The applicable percentages of gross income to be considered by the trier of fact are:

Number of Children	Percentage of Gross Income
1	17-23 percent
2	23-28 percent
3	25-32 percent
4	29-35 percent
5 (or more)	31-37 percent

These guidelines are intended by the General Assembly to guidelines only and any court so applying these guidelines shall not abrogate its responsibility in making the final determination of child support based on the evidence presented to it at the time of trial.

(c) The trier of fact may vary the final award of child support, up or down, outside the range enumerated in paragraph (5) of subsection (b) of this Code section upon a written finding of special circumstances. The special circumstances may be any factor which the trier of fact deems to be required by the ends of justice. Some of the factors which may warrant such variations include, but are not limited to:

(1) Ages of the children.

> (2) A child's medical costs or extraordinary needs.
> (3) Educations costs.
> (4) Day care costs.
> (5) Shared physical custody arrangements that may include extended visitation.
> (6) A party's obligations to another household.
> (7) Income which a spouse could make if they wanted to work.
> (8) Benefits that a spouse is getting which are not included in their salary.
> (9) Additional support, such as payment of a mortgage.
> (10) A spouse's own extraordinary needs, such as significant medical expenses.
> (11) Extreme economic conditions, such as high income (usually over $75,000 gross a year, or very high debt loads).
> (12) An historical pattern of spending on the children that puts the parties out of the general range of support, such as always sending the children to expensive camps or private schools that were not really within the parties means.
> (13) In-kind contributions of the parties.
> (14) The income of the custodial parent.
> (15) Economic factors within the community.

(d) The guidelines shall be reviewed by a commission appointed by the Governor to ensure that their application results in the determination of appropriate child support award amounts. The commission will complete its review and submit its report within four years following July 1, 1989, and shall continue such reviews every four years thereafter. Nothing contained in such report shall be considered to authorize or require a change in the guidelines without action by the General Assembly having the force and effect of law. The commission shall also submit a report to the House Judiciary Committee and Senate Special Judiciary Committee during the 1991 regular session of the General Assembly. This report shall provide information which will allow these committees to review the effectiveness of the guidelines and, if necessary, revise these guidelines.

(e) The duty to provide support for a minor child shall continue until the child reaches the age of majority, dies, marries, or becomes emancipated, whichever first occurs; provided, however, that, in any temporary or final order for child support with respect to any proceeding for divorce, separate maintenance, legitimacy, or paternity entered on or after July 1, 1992, the trier of fact, in the exercise of sound discretion, may direct either or both parents to provide financial assistance to a child who has not previously married or become emancipated, who is enrolled in and attending secondary school, and who has attained the age of majority before completing his or her secondary school education, provided that such financial assistance shall not be required after a child attains 20 years of age. The provisions for support provided in this subsection may be enforced by either parent of the child for whose benefit the support is ordered.

(f) The provisions of subsection (e) of this Code shall be applicable only to a temporary order or final decree for divorce, separate maintenance, legitimation, or paternity entered after July 1, 1992, and the same shall be applicable to an action for modification of a decree entered in such an action entered on or after July 1, 1992, only upon a showing of a significant change or material circumstances.

Appendix C
Forms

Be sure to read "An Introduction to Legal Forms" in chapter 5 before you begin using the forms in this appendix. Instructions for completing the forms are found throughout this book. Instructions for a particular form may be located by looking in the index under "forms, instructions." You will not need to use all of the foms in this appendix. The forms are listed below, both by number and title, and the page number is given where each form begins.

Do not remove forms from this book. Instead, make photocopies to use for both practice worksheets and the forms you will actually file with the court. This allows you to have blank forms in order to make more copies if you make mistakes or need additional copies.

Table of Forms

Where to Find Additional Forms. This book is designed for the most typical divorce situations. In unusual situations there are numerous other forms that can be filed to obtain various results. These include forms for such matters as protection from domestic violence, ordering drug testing, the appointment of a guardian ad litem for your children, counseling and psychological examinations, mediation, preventing the removal of children from the state and denial of passport services, and dismissing a divorce case due a reconciliation with your spouse. There are two basic sources of legal forms. The first is the law library. Ask the librarian where to find divorce form books. There are specific guides to divorce matters that will contain forms, and there are also general legal form books containing forms on all kinds of legal matters. (See chapter 2 on Legal Research for the titles of some of these books.) The second source is the court clerk, who may have standardized forms for certain matters.

PROPERTY INVENTORY

(1) N-M	(2) DESCRIPTION	(3) ID#	(4) VALUE	(5) BALANCE OWED	(6) EQUITY	(7) OWNER H-W-J	(8) H	(9) W

DEBT INVENTORY

(1) N-M	(2) CREDITOR	(3) ACCOUNT NO.	(4) NOTES	(5) MONTHLY PAYMENT	(6) BALANCE OWED	(7) DATE	(8) OWNER H-W-J	(9) H	(10) W

CHILD SUPPORT GUIDELINES WORKSHEET

FATHER: _____   MOTHER: _____

OCCUPATION: _____   OCCUPATION: _____

EMPLOYER: _____   EMPLOYER: _____

SOC. SEC: _____   SOC. SEC: _____

CHILDREN

NAME	DOB	AGE
_____	_____	_____
_____	_____	_____
_____	_____	_____
_____	_____	_____
_____	_____	_____

CHILD SUPPORT CALCULATIONS

PAYING SPOUSE

STEP 1: DETERMINE MONTHLY GROSS INCOME:

1. Actual Gross Income $
    (Schedule A)

2. Imputed Monthly Income $

3. TOTAL GROSS MONTHLY INCOME $
    (Add lines 1 + 2)

STEP 2: MULTIPLY BY THE PERCENTAGE ADJUSTMENT

		HIGH	LOW
4.	Court Guidelines (Schedule A)	$	$
5.	Weekly Obligation (Divided line 4 by 52)	$	$

Schedule A: Child Support Guidelines

To keep from having to make special findings justifying an unconventional decision, you can count on the court using the following percentages:

Number of Children	Percentage of Gross Income
1	17-23 percent
2	23-28 percent
3	25-32 percent
4	29-35 percent
5 (or more)	31-37 percent

To justify an award outside of these guidelines, special circumstances include (but are not limited to):

1) Ages of the children.
2) A child's medical costs or extraordinary needs.
3) Educations costs.
4) Day care costs.
5) Shared physical custody arrangements that may include extended visitation.
6) A party's obligations to another household.
7) Income which a spouse could make if they wanted to work.
8) Benefits that a spouse is getting which are not included in their salary.
9) Additional support, such as payment of a mortgage
10) A spouse's own extraordinary needs, such as significant medical expenses.
11) Extreme economic conditions, such as high income (usually over $75,000 gross a year, or very high debt loads).
12) An historical pattern of spending on the children that puts the parties out of the general range of support, such as always sending the children to expensive camps or private schools that were not really within the parties means.
13) In-kind contributions of the parties.
14) The income of the custodial parent.
15) Economic factors within the community.

IN THE SUPERIOR COURT OF _____ COUNTY
STATE OF GEORGIA

_____

_____   CIVIL ACTION

_____   NUMBER _____

            PLAINTIFF   COST DEPOSIT _____

VS.

_____

_____

_____

            DEFENDANT

SUMMONS

TO THE ABOVE NAMED DEFENDANT:

You are hereby summoned and required to file with the Clerk of said court and serve upon the Plaintiff's attorney, whose name and address is:

an answer to the complaint which is herewith served upon you, within 30 days after service of this summons upon you, exclusive of the day of service. If you fail to do so, judgment by default will be taken against you for the relief demanded in the complaint.

This _____ day of _____, _____

Clerk of Superior Court

By _____
                          Clerk

To Defendant upon whom this petition is served:

This copy of complaint and summons was served upon you _____, _____.

_____
Deputy Sheriff,   County, Georgia

_____COURT OF _____ COUNTY   CASE NUMBER _____

Georgia, _____ County   _____

                                                        Plaintiff

                                    _____
                                                                        vs.

                                    _____
                                                        Defendant

                                    _____
                                                        Address

           Attorney or Plaintiff's Name & Address   _____

                                                        Garnishee

_____   _____

                                                        Address

_____

                                    Designate Party to be served by placing a
                                    check in box above

SHERIFF'S ENTRY OF SERVICE

I have this day served the defendant ....personally with a copy
of the within action and summons.

I have this day served the defendant ....by leaving
a copy of the action and summons at his most notorious place of abode in this County.

Delivered same into hands of .... described as follows
age, about .... years; weight, about .... pounds; height, about ....feet and ....inches,
domiciled at the residence of defendant, at .... A.M. - P.M.

Served the (defendant, Garnishee) .... a corporation
by leaving a copy of the within action and summons with ....
in charge of the office and place of doing business of said Corporation in this County, at .......A.M.-P.M.

I have this day served the above affidavit and summons on the defendant(s) by posting a copy of the same to
the door of the premises designated in said affidavit, and on the same day of such posting by depositing a
true copy of same in the United States Mail, First Class, in an envelope properly addressed to the defendant(s)
at the address shown in said summons, with adequate postage affixed thereon containing notice to the
defendant(s) to answer said summons at the place in the summons.

Diligent search made and defendant ....
not to be found in the jurisdiction of this Court.

The defendant is required to answer no later than .... , ... ,
at the place stated in the summons.

This _____ day of _____, _____

SHERIFF DOCKET _____ Page_____   _____

                                                DEPUTY SHERIFF,   COUNTY.

IN THE SUPERIOR COURT OF _____ COUNTY

STATE OF GEORGIA

_____   *

Plaintiff   *   CIVIL ACTION

vs.   *   FILE #: _____

   *

_____   *

Defendant   *

RULE NISI

The within and foregoing Petition of the Plaintiff [or Defendant] having been read and considered, the matter is set down for a hearing on the issues raised therein before this Court on the _____ day of _____, _____, at _____ o'clock _____ M, or as soon thereafter as the parties may be heard, and the Defendant [or Plaintiffs] ordered and directed to appear at said hearing and to show cause why the prayers of the Plaintiff [or Defendant] should not be granted.

_____

Judge/Clerk _____ Superior Court

Submitted by:

_____

Pro Se

Address and phone number:

_____

_____

_____

_____

I HEREBY CERTIFY THAT I HAVE SERVED THIS _____

_____ ,

UPON _____ , BY

    ❏ HAND DELIVERY

    ❏ DEPOSITING SAME IN THE UNITED STATES MAIL
       IN A PROPERLY ADDRESSED ENVELOPE WITH
       ADEQUATE POSTAGE THEREON.

This _____ , _____

_____

Plaintiff [or Defendant]

Address:

_____

_____

_____

_____

This form must be completed and filed in the Clerk's office before this case can be assigned to a Judge or scheduled for any type hearing.

CLERK OF SUPERIOR COURT
DISCLOSURE STATEMENT

_____
Plaintiff

vs.

_____
Defendant

TYPE OF ACTION

1. ___Divorce without Agreement Attached
2. ___Divorce with Agreement Attached
3. ___Domestic Relations
4. ___Damages arising out of contract
5. ___Damages arising out of tort
6. ___Condemnation
7. ___Equity
8. ___Zoning - County Ordinance violations (i.e. Injunctive relief-zoning)
9. ___Zoning Appeals (denovo)
10. ___Appeal, including denovo appeal excluding Zoning

11. ___URESA
12. ___Name Change
13. ___Other

PREVIOUS RELATED CASES

Does this case involved substantially the same parties, or substantially the same subject matter, or substantially to same factual issues, as any other case filed in this court? (Whether pending simultaneously or not).

_____ NO
_____ YES - If yes, please fill out the following:
    1. Case # _____
    2. Parties _____ vs. _____
    3. Assigned Judge _____
    4. Is this case still pending? _____ Yes _____ No
    5. Brief description of similarities:

_____
_____

_____
Attorney or Party Filing Suit

FOR CLERK'S OFFICE USE ONLY
      CASE # _____

165

CIVIL CASE INITIATION FORM

(Please type or print legibly)

SUPERIOR COURT

_____ COUNTY

GEORGIA

DATE FILED ☐☐ — ☐☐ — ☐☐

PLAINTIFF(S) (Last Name, First, Middle Initial)

_____
_____
_____
_____

ATTORNEY(S) (Name, Address, Phone, Bar#)

_____
_____
_____
_____

FOR OFFICIAL USE ONLY
CASE NUMBER

☐☐☐☐☐☐☐☐ — ☐☐

DATE OF FIRST SERVICE

☐☐ — ☐☐ — ☐☐

DEFENDANT(S) (Last Name, First, Middle Initial)

_____
_____
_____
_____

ATTORNEY(S) (Name, Address, Phone, Bar#)

_____
_____
_____
_____

CAUSE OF ACTION
(Please check an action)

❑ ADOPTION (001)

❑ DIVORCE/ALIMONY (002)

❑ SUPPORT/CUSTODY (003)

❑ MODIFICATIONS (004)

❑ FAMILY VIOLENCE (005)

❑ LEGITIMATION (006)

❑ CONTEMPT (007)

❑ CONTRACT/ACCOUNT (008)

❑ TORT/NEGLIGENCE (009)

❑ HABEAS CORPUS (010)

❑ APPEALS/REVIEW (011)

❑ TITLE TO LAND/
CONDEMNATION (012)

❑ POST-JUDGMENT GARNISHMENT/
ATTACHMENT (013)

❑ CONDEMNATION/FORECLOSURE
(PERSONAL PROPERTY) (014)

❑ DISPOSSESSORY/DISTRESS (015)

❑ NON-DOMESTIC CONTEMPT (016)

❑ DOMESTICATION OF FOREIGN
JUDGMENT (017)

❑ OTHER CAUSE OF ACTION (Cite Ga. statute or give brief description) (018)

CIVIL CASE DISPOSITION FORM

(Please type or print legibly)

SUPERIOR COURT

| FOR OFFICIAL USE ONLY |
| CASE NUMBER |
| — |

_____ COUNTY

GEORGIA

ATTORNEY(S) (Name, Address, Phone, Bar#)

_____

_____

DISPOSITION DATE

PRE-TRIAL DISPOSITIONS	BENCH TRIAL	JURY TRIAL
For: ❏ Plaintiff	For: ❏ Plaintiff	For: ❏ Plaintiff
❏ Defendant	❏ Defendant	❏ Defendant

PRE-TRIAL DISPOSITIONS

❏ SETTLED/DISMISSED (001)

❏ DEFAULT JUDGMENT (002)

❏ SUMMARY JUDGMENT (003)

❏ CONSENT JUDGMENT (004)

❏ JUDGMENT ON PLEADINGS (005)

❏ OTHER PRE-TRIAL (006)

❏ OTHER PRE-TRIAL (006)

(Please specify) _____

BENCH TRIAL

❏ JUDGMENT FOR PLAINTIFF/ DEFENDANT (007)
(Record a bench trial when the parties appear before a judge who hears issues and evidence, including testimony, then makes a determination without a jury.)

JURY TRIAL

❏ JUDGMENT ON VERDICT (008)

❏ DIRECTED VERDICT (009)

❏ JUDGMENT N/W VERDICT (010)

IN THE SUPERIOR COURT OF _____ COUNTY
STATE OF GEORGIA

_____

<table>
<tr><td>Plaintiff</td><td>CIVIL ACTION</td></tr>
<tr><td>vs.</td><td>FILE #: _____</td></tr>
</table>

_____

Defendant

PETITION FOR DIVORCE

Comes now, Plaintiff in the above-styled action and files this Petition for Divorce against Defendant and respectfully shows the Court the following:

1.

Plaintiff _____has been a resident of the State of Georgia, and county of _____ for more than six months immediately preceding the filing of this action.

2.

❑ Defendant _____ is a resident of the State of Georgia, and has consented to the jurisdiction of this Court and has acknowledged service of process and jurisdiction and venue of this Court are correct.

[or]

❑ Defendant _____ may be served at Defendant's residence address of _____, and is subject to the jurisdiction and venue of this Court.

3.

Plaintiff and Defendant were married on or about _____, _____, and lived together as Husband and Wife until on or about _____, _____, when they separated, and they have remained in a bona fide state of separation since that date.

4.

❏   There are no children as issue of this marriage.

❏   The child(ren) as issue of this marriage, are:

Name   Age   Date of Birth

The Petitioner is employed with _____, and earns approximately $_____ per year. The Respondent is employed with _____ _____and earns approximately $_____ per year.

5.

❏   There is no undivided marital property as evidenced by the settlement agreement between the parties hereto, and the plaintiff prays the agreement be made the order of the court.

❏   The Plaintiff seeks the following: [choose which items are appropriate]

   ❏   Temporary and permanent child support;

   ❏   Temporary and permanent alimony;

   ❏   An equitable division of the assets and liabilities of the parties;

   ❏   Costs incurred in bringing this action.

6.

Plaintiff brings this divorce on the grounds that the marriage is irretrievably broken, as defined by Georgia law.

7.

The Wife desires the restoration of her maiden name, to wit: _____.

WHEREFORE, the Plaintiff prays:

(a)   That a date be set for a hearing on the claims of the parties, and that process issue if required;

(b)   That Plaintiff be granted a total divorce, that is a divorce a vinculo matrimonii;

(c)   That the Plaintiff be given relief as sought, or that any agreement between the parties hereto be made a part of any final decree issued by the Court;

(d)   That Plaintiff and Defendant receive such other relief as the Court deems just and equitable.

This _____, _____.

_____
Plaintiff, Pro Se

Name and address

_____
_____
_____
_____

STATE OF GEORGIA   *

                                   *

COUNTY OF _____   *

VERIFICATION

PERSONALLY appeared before the undersigned attesting officer authorized by law to administer oaths, _____, who, being first duly sworn, on oath depose and says that the facts alleged in the above and foregoing Complaint for Divorce are true and correct.

Sworn to and subscribed before me
this _____, _____

_____
Notary Public

DOMESTIC RELATIONS FINANCIAL AFFIDAVIT

1. AFFIANT'S NAME:_____ Age:_____ SSN:_____

    SPOUSE'S NAME: _____ Age:_____ SSN:_____

    Date of marriage:_____ Date of Separation:_____ No. of marriages: H___ W___

    Names and birth dates of children of this marriage:

Name	Date of Birth	Resides With

    Names and birth dates of children of prior marriage residing with Affiant:

Name	Date of Birth

2. SUMMARY OF AFFIANT'S INCOME AND NEEDS

    (a) Gross monthly income (from Item 3A) $_____

    (b) Net monthly income (from Item 3C)   _____

    (c) Average monthly expenses (Item 5A)   _____

        Monthly payments to creditors (Item 5B)   _____

        Total monthly expenses and payments to creditors (Item 5C)   _____

    (d) Amount of spousal/child support needed by affiant   _____

    (e) Amount of child support indicated by Child Sup't Guidelines $_____

3. A. AFFIANT'S GROSS MONTHLY INCOME

    (All income must be entered based on monthly average regardless of date of receipt. Where applicable, income should be annualized.)

    Salary $_____

    Bonuses, commissions, allowances, overtime, tips and similar payments (based on past 12-month average or time of employment if < than 1 year)

    ATTACH SHEET ITEMIZING THIS INCOME $_____

    Business income from sources such as self employment, partnership, close corporations and/or independent contracts (gross receipts minus ordinary and necessary expenses required to produce income)

    ATTACH SHEET ITEMIZING THIS INCOME $_____

    Disability/unemployment/worker's compensation $_____

    Pension, retirements or annuity payments   _____

    Social security benefits   _____

    Other public benefits (specify)   _____

    Spousal or child support from prior marriage   _____

    Interest and dividends   _____

    Rental income (gross receipts minus ordinary and necessary expenses required to produce income) ATTACH SHEET ITEMIZING THIS INCOME.   _____

    Income from royalties, trusts or estates   _____

    Gains derived from dealing in property (except non-recurring)   _____

    Other income of a recurring type (specify source)   _____

    GROSS MONTHLY INCOME $_____

    B. List and describe all benefits of employment, e.g., automobile and/or auto allowance, insurance (auto, life, disability, etc.), deferred compensation, employer contribution to retirement or stock, club memberships and reimbursed expenses (to the extent they reduce personal living expenses) ATTACH SHEET, IF NEEDED. $_____

    _____

    _____

    C. Net monthly income from employment (deduct only state and federal taxes and FICA). $_____

    Affiant's pay period: (ie., weekly, monthly)_____ No. exemptions_____

4.   ASSETS (If you claim or agree that all or part of an asset is non-marital, indicate the non-marital portion under the appropriate spouse's column. The total value of each asset must be listed in the "value" column. "Value" means what you feel the item of property would be worth if it were offered for sale.)

Description	Value	Separate Asset of Husband	Separate Asset of Wife
Cash	$_____	_____	_____
Stocks, bonds	_____	_____	_____
CD's/Money Mkt. Acct.	_____	_____	_____
Real estate: Home	_____	_____	_____
Other	_____	_____	_____
Automobiles	_____	_____	_____
Money owed you	_____	_____	_____
Retirement/IRA	_____	_____	_____
Furniture/furnishings	_____	_____	_____
Jewelry	_____	_____	_____
Life ins. (cash value)	_____	_____	_____
Collectibles	_____	_____	_____
Bank accounts	_____	_____	_____
(list each acct)	_____	_____	_____
Other assets	_____	_____	_____
TOTAL ASSETS	$_____	$_____	$_____

5. A. AVERAGE MONTHLY EXPENSES
HOUSEHOLD

Mortgage or rent payments	$_____
Property taxes	_____
Insurance	_____
Electricity	_____
Water	_____
Garbage & sewer	_____
Telephone	_____
Gas	_____
Repairs & maintenance	_____
Lawn care	_____
Pest control	_____
Cable TV	_____
Misc. household & grocery	_____
Meals outside home	_____
Other	_____

AFFIANT'S OTHER EXPENSES

Dry cleaning and laundry	_____
Clothing	_____
Medical/dental	_____
Prescriptions	_____
Affiant's gifts	_____
Entertainment	_____
Vacations	_____
Publications, dues, clubs	_____
Religious and charities	_____
Miscellaneous (attach sheet)	_____

Other (attach sheet)	_____
Alimony paid to former spouse	_____

CHILDREN'S EXPENSES

Child care	_____
School tuition	_____
School supplies/expenses	_____
Lunch money	_____
Allowance	_____
Clothing	_____
Diapers	_____
Medical/dental Rx	_____
Grooming/hygiene	_____
Gifts	_____
Entertainment	_____
Activities	_____

OTHER INSURANCE

Health	_____
Life	_____
Disability	_____
Other	_____

AUTOMOBILE

Gasoline and oil	_____
Repairs	_____
Auto tags and license	_____
Insurance	_____
TOTAL ABOVE EXPENSES	$_____

B. PAYMENTS TO CREDITORS (Attach sheet if necessary)

To Whom	(Incl. acct#)	Balance Due	Monthly Payment
_____	_____	_____	_____
_____	_____	_____	_____
_____	_____	_____	_____
_____	_____	_____	_____
Total Monthly Payments to Creditors		$_____	$_____

C.   TOTAL MONTHLY EXPENSES $_____

This _____ day of _____, _____

_____   _____
Notary Public   Affiant

IN THE SUPERIOR COURT OF _____ COUNTY

STATE OF GEORGIA

_____

Plaintiff

CIVIL ACTION

vs.

FILE #:

_____

Defendant

AGREEMENT

This Agreement is made and entered into by and between Plaintiff and Defendant.

WITNESSETH:

WHEREAS, the parties hereto are Husband and Wife, having gotten married _____, _____; and

WHEREAS, the parties hereto have lived in a bona fide state of separation since on or about _____, _____; and

WHEREAS, without agreeing in any sense to a divorce, said parties hereto desire to settle between themselves certain issues, including alimony, and the division of property between them;

NOW THEREFORE, the said parties hereto, for and in consideration of the promises and recitals herein contained, do mutually agree and promise as follows:

1. CHILD CUSTODY & VISITATION

❏ There are no minor children as issue of this marriage and there is no issue of child custody or visitation.

❏ The   ❏ Plaintiff   ❏ Defendant shall have temporary and permanent custody and control of the minor child(ren) being issue of this marriage, and shall be denominated as the "Custodial Parent." The other party shall be denominated as the "Non-Custodial Parent," and shall have the right of reasonable and liberal visitation with said child at times and places to be agreed upon by the parties, unless more specific visitation provisions are set forth in this Agreement.

❏ The Plaintiff and Defendant shall share "Joint Custody" of the minor child, however, the ❏ Plaintiff ❏ Defendant shall have temporary and permanent primary legal and physical custody and control of the minor child being issue of this marriage, and shall be denominated the "Primary Custodial Parent." The other party shall The Defendant shall be denominated as the "Secondary Custodial Parent," and shall have the right of reasonable and liberal visitation with said child at times and places to be agreed upon by the parties, unless more specific visitation provisions are set forth in this Agreement.

SPECIFIC VISITATION PROVISIONS: The parties agree to the following provisions for visitation by the Non-Custodial Parent:

Standard Visitation Language

Visitation The visitation of the Non-Custodial Parent shall be at such place of his or her choice, and such visitation shall be reasonable and liberal, but in the event that the parties are unable to agree to such visitation the agreed upon schedule shall be as follows:

(a) During the first and third weekends of each month from Friday at 6:00 p.m. until Sunday at 6:00 p.m. provided that the Non-Custodial Parent shall give the Custodial Parent at least 24 hours advance notice, written or oral, of any intention to exercise this right;

(b) For any four (4) weeks during summer vacation so long as the Non-Custodial Parent does not interfere with or interrupt any of the child's school and further provided that the Non-Custodial Parent shall give the Custodial Parent at least (14) days advance notice, written or oral, of each summer visitation;

(c) During even-number years, the Thanksgiving holiday, from 6:00 p.m. on the Wednesday before Thanksgiving to 6:00 p.m. on the Sunday following Thanksgiving, and the New Years holiday from December 27, at 6:00 p.m. to January 1, at 6:00 p.m., provided that the Non-Custodial Parent shall give the Custodial Parent at least fourteen (14) days advance notice of each intended visitation;

(d) During odd-numbered years, the Christmas holiday from December 23, at 6:00 p.m. to December 27, at 6:00 p.m; the spring vacation specified by the child's school district, from the first day at 6:00 p.m. to the 7th day at 6:00 p.m. (the Custodial Parent shall give the Non-Custodial Parent thirty (30) days notice as to the specified dates of the spring vacation); and the children's birthdays, from 6:00 p.m. of the day preceding until 6:00 p.m. of birthday; all provided that the Non-Custodial Parent shall give the Custodial Parent fourteen (14) days advance notice of each intended visitation;

(e) The Non-Custodial Parent shall be responsible for transportation and promptness in each visitation. For each visitation, the Non-Custodial Parent shall receive the children at the residence of the Custodial Parent, and after such visitation, shall return the child to the residence of the Custodial Parent.

Visitation in the Event of Geographical Separation Notwithstanding the aforementioned, should the parties be domiciled more than one hundred miles apart, and the minor child be above the age of three years, the following minimum visitation shall apply:

(a) The Non-Custodial Parent shall be entitled to four days regular visitation per month. In no event shall the monthly four days be cumulative, nor shall the four days of regular visitation in any one month exceed ninety-six consecutive hours.

(b) In addition, the Non-Custodial Parent shall be entitled to six weeks of visitation to take place during the Summer, or contemporaneously with the child's vacation, that may be exercised during any calendar year. The purpose of this visitation is to allow the Non-Custodial Parent extended time with the minor child. This vacation visitation shall not exceed forty-two consecutive days per visit, and shall be in lieu of the regular visitation for the months in which vacation visitation is exercised. In the event that vacation visitation bridges two months, it shall be in lieu of the regular visitation for both months.

(c) The Non-Custodial Parent shall be responsible for the expenses of transporting the minor child to the residence of the Non-Custodial Parent and the Custodial Parent shall be responsible for the expenses of returning the child to the residence of the Custodial Parent.

(d) In the event that either parent moves more than 500 miles from the present marital residence in then the primary residence of the children shall be with the non-moving parent who shall become the Custodial parent if he or she is not already so designated and the parent who has moved more than 500 miles or to another city in another state will have the same visitation rights with the child as are previously defined.

2. ACCESS AND DECISIONS

The parties agree that the Non-Custodial Parent shall be entitled to equal access to all teachers, schools, counselors, psychologists, physicians, and dentists of said child and agree further that the Custodial Parent shall provide the Non-Custodial Parent with copies of the child's report cards, and progress reports as received. Although the Non-Custodial Parent shall have a voice in all major decisions concerning said child's education and upbringing, the Custodial Parent shall have the ultimate right and responsibility to decide substantial issues including but not limited to where said child will live and what schools will be attended. In the event of any disagreement regarding same, the Custodial Parent's decisions shall prevail.

3. COMMUNICATIONS WITH CHILDREN

The parties mutually agree that is of great importance that the children of the parties be taught and encouraged to love and respect both of their parents. The parties therefore covenant that neither will make derogatory remarks about the other in the presence of the children; that each will notify the other of any illness of the children; that each shall cooperate and work together to encourage and assist the child in attaining the highest possible educational levels and achievements; and that the parties will work with one another towards helping the child overcome any problems which may arise the child's life.

4. CHILD SUPPORT

❑ There is no issue of child support.

❑ The Non-Custodial Parent shall pay to the Custodial Parent the sum of $_____ per _____ from the date of Agreement until the minor child has attained the age of eighteen, dies, marries or becomes self-supporting, unless the child is still enrolled full time in secondary school, however, support under this paragraph shall not continue past the child's twentieth birthday. The parties testify that this sum represents _____% of the Non-Custodial Parent's gross income, and falls within the parameters required by the Uniform Superior Court guidelines for child support.

❑ The parent receiving support shall have the right to submit an income deduction order at his or her sole election.

❑ The parties further agree to the following provisions regarding child support:

5. ALIMONY

❑ Both parties waive any claim for alimony against the other including any claim for retirement benefits to which either may be entitled.

❑ The ❑ Plaintiff ❑ Defendant shall pay to the other party the sum of $_____ dollars a week/month/year, for a period of _____ consecutive weeks/months/years, or unless said recipient of alimony remarries or dies, at which time the alimony obligation shall cease.

❑ The parties further agree to the following provisions regarding alimony:

6. DIVISION OF PROPERTY

All of the property which the parties presently own jointly or severally, whether real, personal, or mixed, and of whatever kind or nature and wheresoever situated, and all property in which either has any interest, shall be divided as follows:

(a) <u>Real Property:</u>

❑ The parties own no real property.

❑ The parties own a parcel of real property in _____ County, Georgia, being _____.

The parties agree that the _____ shall be the sole owner, free and clear of any claim of the _____ of the property and shall be fully responsible therefor. Within forty-eight hours of an order being entered, the _____ will execute a Quit Claim Deed in favor of the _____.

❑ The parties own a parcel of real property in _____ County, Georgia, being _____.

The parties agree that said property shall be sold and the proceeds shall be divided equally between parties.

(b) <u>Personal Property:</u> Each party shall have possession of and title to all those personal items presently in their respective possession, and shall be responsible for any indebtedness associated with same.

(c) <u>Household Goods:</u> All furniture and household goods have been previously divided between the parties, and each shall retain and have title to such furniture and household goods as are in their respective possessions and shall be responsible for any indebtedness associated with same.

(d) <u>Cash:</u> All cash presently in the possession of either party shall be and remain their separate property, free and clear of any claim whatsoever on the part of the other party.

(e) <u>Bank Accounts and Investments:</u> All bank accounts and investments have been previously divided between the parties, and each shall retain and have title to bank accounts and investments as are in their respective possessions. All other joint accounts whether saving or checking have been closed, and the funds therein apportioned between the parties.

(f) <u>Automobiles, Boats, Etc.</u> The Plaintiff shall be the sole owner, free and clear of any claim of the Defendant of the _____, VIN# _____, and shall be fully responsible therefor. The Defendant shall be the sole owner, free and clear of any claim of the Plaintiff, of the _____, VIN # _____. Each party shall retain title to such other vehicles as are in their own names, and shall be fully responsible therefor.

All of the other property which the parties presently own jointly or severally, whether real, personal, or mixed, and of whatever kind or nature and wheresoever situated, and all property in which either has any interest has been previously divided and the property belonging to each is in his or her possession and control.

7. INSURANCE

❑ The parties agree to provide for their own health insurance, and neither shall have any responsibility for any insurance with respect to the other. Any disposition of any other life insurance policies currently in force shall be at the sole discretion of the individual owner of said policy. The parties shall each be responsible for their own medical and dental insurance. Any coverage currently in force and offered through an employer shall be maintained pursuant to COBRA by the Defendant and in favor of the Plaintiff.

❑ The Non-Custodial Parent shall keep the minor child insured under such medical, dental and hospitalization plans as may be available through the employer. Any necessary medical, dental, or related health care expenses not covered by such insurance shall be borne equally by the parties. Any such medical bills submitted to one party by the other, and which have been paid by the other party, shall be reimbursed within thirty days of receipt.

8. SEPARATE RIGHTS

From and after the date of this Agreement, the parties hereto shall have the right to live separate, undisturbed, and apart from each other.

9. DEBTS

The parties agree to each be responsible for their own obligations and have previously apportioned all joint obligations. Each party's assumption of debt and indemnification is an integral part of the support agreement in that if said assumption and indemnification had not taken place, the amount of spousal support would have been different in order to provide the support necessary to ensure that the daily needs of the Wife [and Children] are satisfied. Therefore, the assumption of debt and indemnification in this agreement shall not be considered dischargeable in any bankruptcy proceeding by either party as against the other.

The Wife shall specifically be responsible for the following obligations:

Name   Account Number   Amount

_____

_____

_____

The Husband shall specifically be responsible for the following obligations:

Name   Account Number   Amount

_____

_____

_____

10. TAXES

The parties agree to file ❑ individual ❑ joint income tax returns for _____ and to be individually responsible for their own tax liabilities thereafter. The parties shall equally share for any joint accrued tax liability from the years prior to _____ .

The ❏ Plaintiff ❏ Defendant shall be responsible for any accrued tax liability for the period of _____, _____, to _____, _____.

The Custodial Parent shall be entitled to claim the child(ren) of the parties for federal and state income tax purposes, however, in the event of any agreement to the contrary, the Non-Custodial Parent shall only be entitled to claim the child(ren) with a written consent from the Custodial Parent in compliance with Federal guidelines, and only if the Non-Custodial Parent is current on all other obligations created under this Agreement.

11. KNOWLEDGE OF CONTENTS

Each party expressly acknowledges that he or she has read this Agreement in its entirety prior to the execution thereof, understands the provisions thereof, executes this Agreement as his or her voluntary act, and that there are no agreements or promises between the parties except as herein set forth. Both parties consent to this Agreement being made a part of the Final Judgment and Decree of the Court in the divorce action to be filed in the Superior Court of this County, if said divorce is granted by the Court.

12. MODIFICATION

Any modification or waiver of any of the provisions of this Agreement shall be effective only if made in writing and executed by both parties with the same formality as this Agreement. The failure of either party to insist upon strict compliance with any of the provisions of this Agreement shall not be construed as a waiver of any subsequent default of the same or similar nature.

13. FULL SETTLEMENT

This Agreement shall constitute a full and final settlement of all claims of every nature between the parties hereto.

14. AGREEMENT TO TRY

The parties agree that the divorce action filed in conjunction with this Agreement may be tried at any time after thirty-one (31) days from the date of service of the Complaint for Divorce.

15. EFFECTIVE DATE

This Agreement shall become effective on the date of the execution hereof by the parties hereto.

16. ENFORCEMENT

Each of the parties hereto shall strictly obey and abide by each and every term and provision of this Agreement. Upon this Agreement's being incorporated in any Order of any Court, and in the event then of any breach of this Agreement, the offending party shall be subject to attachment for contempt and garnishment of any alimony or child support award.

17. WAIVER OF DISCOVERY

Each party acknowledges their right to discovery as provided by the Georgia Civil Practice Act and desires not to proceed with discovery.

18. ATTORNEYS

The parties agree that each shall be responsible for their own incurred attorney's fees and neither shall have any responsibility with respect to fees incurred by the other. Each party has either had this Agreement carefully explained to them by counsel, or has explicitly chosen not to avail themselves of that right despite opportunity and encouragement to so do.

IN WITNESS WHEREOF, the parties hereto have hereunto set their hands and seals, and affirmed the contents and veracity of the statements contained herein this

_____, _____.

_____   _____
PLAINTIFF   DEFENDANT

Sworn to and subscribed before me this

_____day of _____, _____.

_____
Notary Public

Sworn to and subscribed before me this

_____day of _____, _____.

_____
Notary Public

IN THE SUPERIOR COURT OF _____ COUNTY

STATE OF GEORGIA

_____
Plaintiff   CIVIL ACTION

vs.

                                   FILE #: _____

_____
Defendant

AFFIDAVIT REGARDING CUSTODY

Pursuant to the requirements of the O.C.G.A. § 19-9-49, the Petitioner gives the following information under oath:

1.

The minor child(ren) of the parties is/are

Name	Age	Birthdate	Living With	Address
_____	__	_____	_____	_____
_____	__	_____	_____	_____
_____	__	_____	_____	_____
_____	__	_____	_____	_____
_____	__	_____	_____	_____

2.

The forenamed minor children have, for the past five years, resided with the parties at the following addresses:

1. _____.

2. _____.

3.

Petitioner has not participated as a party, witness, or in any other capacity in any other litigation concerning the custody of the named children in this or any other state, unless indicated below:

4.

Petitioner has no information of any custody proceeding concerning the children in a Court of this or any other state, unless indicated below:

5.

Petitioner knows of no other person not a party to this proceeding who has physical custody of the children or claims to have custody or visitation rights with respect to the children, unless indicated below:

_____
Plaintiff

Sworn to and subscribed before me this
_____ day of _____, _____.

_____
Notary Public

IN THE SUPERIOR COURT OF _____ **COUNTY**
STATE OF GEORGIA

_____

Plaintiff	CIVIL ACTION
vs.	FILE #: _____

_____

Defendant

ANSWER AND COUNTERCLAIM

COMES NOW Defendant in the above styled action and files this, Answer and Counterclaim to the Plaintiff's Complaint, as follows:

1.

Defendant admits the allegations contained in Plaintiff's Complaint.

COUNTERCLAIM

COMES NOW Defendant herein and files her Counterclaim, showing to the Court the following:

1.

Plaintiff is subject to the jurisdiction of this Court.

2.

The marriage of the parties is irretrievably broken and Defendant is entitled to a total divorce from Plaintiff.

3.

Defendant files this counterclaim for the limited purpose of securing the restoration of her former name, to wit: _____.

WHEREFORE, Defendant prays:

(a) That Defendant be awarded a total divorce from Plaintiff, that is to say, a divorce
a vinculo matrimonii;

(b) That Defendant be restored to her maiden name, to wit:

_____.

(c) That Plaintiff have such other and further relief as to the Court may seem meet
and proper.

_____

Pro Se Defendant

Address

_____

_____

_____

_____   NO._____

                    VERSUS   SUPERIOR COURT
                                              _____COUNTY, GEORGIA

_____

FINAL JUDGMENT AND DECREE

Upon consideration of this case, upon evidence submitted as provided by law, it is the judgment of the Court that a total divorce be granted, that is to say, a divorce *a vinculo matrimonii*, between the parties to the above stated case upon legal principles.

It is considered, ordered, and decreed by the Court that the marriage contract heretofore entered into between the parties to this case, from and after this date, be and is set aside and dissolved as fully and effectually as if no such contract had ever been made or entered into.

Petitioner and respondent, formerly husband and wife, in the future shall be held and considered as separate and distinct persons altogether unconnected by any nuptial union or civil contract, whatsoever, and both shall have the right to remarry.

The settlement agreement between the parties, dated _____, is incorporated herein.

The costs of these proceedings are taxed against the _____.

Decree entered this _____ day of _____, _____

                                    _____
                                    Judge, Superior Court
                                    County, Georgia

IN THE SUPERIOR COURT OF _____ COUNTY
STATE OF GEORGIA

_____
Petitioner/Plaintiff

vs.

_____
Respondent/Defendant

Civil Action File Number

_____

FINAL JUDGMENT AND DECREE OF DIVORCE

Upon consideration of this case, upon evidence submitted as provided by law, it is the judgment of this court that a total divorce be granted, that is to say, a divorce *a vinculo matrimonii*, between the parties to the above-stated case upon legal principles.

It is considered, ordered and decreed by the court that the marriage contract heretofore entered into between the parties to this case, from and after this date, be and is set aside and dissolved as fully and effectually as if no such contract had ever been made or entered into.

Petitioner and respondent in the future shall be held and considered as separate and distinct persons altogether unconnected by any nuptial union or civil contract whatsoever and both shall have the right to remarry.

1.

The court restores to (Plaintiff/Defendant) his/her prior maiden name, to wit:
_____.

2.

The settlement Agreement entered into between the parties and filed with the court on _____, is hereby incorporated into and made a part of this Final Judgment and Decree of Divorce.

3.

In determining child support, the court finds as follows:
The gross income of the father is $_____ monthly.
The gross income of the mother is $_____ monthly.
In this case, child support is being determined for ____children.
The applicable percentage of gross income to be considered is:

# of children	Percentage range of gross income
1	17 percent to 23 percent
2	23 percent to 28 percent
3	25 percent to 32 percent
4	29 percent to 35 percent
5	31 percent to 37 percent

Thus, _____ percent of $_____ (gross income of obligor) equals
$_____per month.

The court has considered the existence of special circumstances and has found the following special circumstances marked with an "X" to be present in this case:

_____ 1. Ages of the children.

_____ 2. A child's extraordinary medical costs or needs in addition to accident and sickness insurance, provided that all such costs or needs shall be considered if no insurance is available.

_____ 3. Educational costs.

_____ 4. Day-care costs.

_____ 5. Shared physical custody arrangements, including extended visitation.

_____ 6. A party's other support obligations to another household.

_____ 7. Income that should be imputed to a party because of suppression of income.

_____ 8. In-kind income for the self-employed, such as reimbursed meals or a company car

_____ 9. Other support a party is providing or will be providing, such as payment of mortgage.

_____10. A party's own extraordinary needs, such as medical expenses.

_____11. Extreme economic circumstances, including but not limited to:
(A) Unusually high debt structure; or
(B) Unusually high income of either party or both parties, which shall be construed as individual gross income of over $75,000.00 per annum.

_____ 12. Historical spending in the family for children which varies significantly from the percentage table.

_____ 13. Consideration of the economic cost of living factors of the community of each party, as determined by the trier of fact.

_____ 14. In-kind contribution of either parent.

_____ 15. The income of the custodial parent.

_____ 16. The cost of accident and sickness insurance coverage for dependent children included in this Order.

_____ 17. Extraordinary travel expenses to exercise visitation or shared physical custody.

_____ 18. Any other factor which the trier of fact deems to be required by the ends of justice, as described below:

4.

A. Having found that no special circumstances exist, or that special circumstances numbered _____ exist, the final award of child support which Plaintiff/Defendant shall pay to Plaintiff/Defendant for support of the child or children is $_____ per week/month, beginning on the _____ day of_____, _____, and payable thereafter on the _____ and day of each week/month. Plaintiff/Defendant shall continue to pay child support for the benefit of each child of the parties until each such child becomes 18 years of age, dies, marries, or otherwise becomes emancipated, except that if the child becomes eighteen (18) years of age while enrolled in and attending secondary school on a full-time basis, then such support shall/shall not continue until the child completes secondary school, provided that such support shall not be required after the child attains twenty (20) years of age.

B. Plaintiff/Defendant is ordered to provide accident and sickness insurance for the child or children so long as he or she is obligated by this Order to provide child support for each such child or children.

5.

In accordance with O.C.G.A. § 19-6-32(a.1),

_____ Alimony and Support Unit and Income Deduction Orders are entered contemporaneously with the entry of this Final Judgment and Decree requiring the immediate withholding of child support from the wages of the parent required by this Order to furnish support; or

_____ No Income Deduction Order(s) accompany this Final Judgment and Decree as:

_____ The parent required to furnish support is self-employed; or

_____ An Order or Consent Order for income deduction of child support is already in place; or

_____ "[B]oth parties...have reached ... (a) written agreement...which provides for an alternative arrangement." O.C.G.A. § 19-6-32(a.1)(B) (Supp. 1994).

6.

WHENEVER IN VIOLATION OF THE TERMS OF THIS ORDER THERE SHALL HAVE BEEN A FAILURE TO MAKE THE SUPPORT PAYMENTS DUE HEREUNDER SO THAT THE AMOUNT UNPAID IS EQUAL TO OR GREATER THAN THE AMOUNT PAYABLE FOR ONE (1) MONTH, THE PAYMENTS REQUIRED TO BE MADE MAY BE COLLECTED BY THE PROCESS OF CONTINUING GARNISHMENT FOR SUPPORT. O.C.G.A. § 19-6-30(a) (Supp. 1994).

7.

ADD HERE THE PROPERTY DIVISION PARAGRAPHS

SO ORDERED, this the _____ day of _____, _____.

_____
JUDGE, SUPERIOR COURT

Prepared by:

_____

_____

_____

Name, address, phone

191

IN THE SUPERIOR COURT OF _____ COUNTY

STATE OF GEORGIA

_____

Plaintiff   CIVIL ACTION

vs.   FILE #: _____

_____

Defendant

REQUEST FOR PRODUCTION OF DOCUMENTS

To:

GREETINGS:

    You are requested to produce, pursuant to O.C.G.A. § 9-11-34 (c), the documents and records set forth below for inspection and copying by the [Plaintiff] [Defendant] at

_____

_____, on or before the 30th day after service of this request, where adequate facilities are available for copying. Alternately, you may provide copies of documents requested on or before the expiration of the aforesaid thirty days.

This _____, _____.

                                     _____

                                     [Plaintiff] [Defendant]
                                     Address

                                     _____

                                     _____

                                     _____

                                     Phone_____

I HEREBY CERTIFY THAT I HAVE SERVED THIS REQUEST FOR PRODUCTION TO ALL OTHER PARTIES, (AND/OR WHERE APPROPRIATE, THEIR ATTORNEY(S)) BY EITHER HAND DELIVERY OR DEPOSITING SAME IN THE UNITED STATES MAIL IN A PROPERLY ADDRESSED ENVELOPE WITH ADEQUATE POSTAGE THEREON.

This _____, _____

_____

[Plaintiff] [Defendant]

Address

_____

_____

_____

Phone_____

IN THE SUPERIOR COURT OF _____ COUNTY
STATE OF GEORGIA

_____

<table>
<tr><td>Plaintiff</td><td>CIVIL ACTION</td></tr>
<tr><td>vs.</td><td>FILE #:_____</td></tr>
</table>

_____

Defendant

AFFIDAVIT OF PUBLICATION AND DILIGENT SEARCH

Comes now the Plaintiff who states on oath that diligent search has been made and that the Defendant cannot be found. The Plaintiff has made the following effort to find the Defendant:

_____

_____

_____

_____

However, the Defendant cannot be located and the Plaintiff asks this Court to enter an Order for Publication in the within and foregoing action.

This _____, _____

_____
Affiant's Signature

Sworn to and subscribed before me
this _____, _____

Name _____

Address _____

_____

_____
Notary Public

Telephone _____

ORDER OF PUBLICATION

STATE OF GEORGIA
COUNTY OF _____

It appearing to the satisfaction of the court by Affidavit, that _____,
a defendant on whom service is to be made in Case Number _____, _____
resides out of the State, or has departed from the State, or cannot after due diligence, be found within the State, or conceals (him) (her) self to avoid service of the Summons, and it further appearing, either by Affidavit or by verified Complaint on file, that a claim exists against the defendant in respect to whom service is to be made, and that (he) (she) is a necessary or proper party to the action,

IT IS HEREBY CONSIDERED, ORDERED AND DECREED THAT:

(1) Service be perfected by publication to be made in the paper in which sheriff's advertisements are printed four times within the ensuing sixty (60) days, publications to be at least (7) days apart.

(2) The party obtaining the Order for Publication deposit or pay, at the time of filing to cost of publication.

(3) Said notice shall contain (a) the name of the parties - plaintiff and defendant (b) a caption setting forth the court (c) the character of the action (d) the date the action was filed (e) the date of the Order for Service By Publication (f) notice directed and addressed to the party to be served commanding him to file with _____,
the Clerk and serve upon the plaintiff's attorney, an Answer in writing within sixty (60) days from the date of this Order for Publication (g) teste in the name of the Judge, and (h) the signature of _____, the Clerk of _____ Superior Court.

(4) Where the residence or abiding place of said absent or nonresident party is known, the party obtaining the Order shall advise _____, the Clerk, who shall, within fifteen (15) days after filing the Order for service by Publication, enclose, direct, stamp and mail a copy of this order for Service By Publication and Complaint (if any) to said Party at his last known address, if any and make entry of his actions.

(5) The copy of the notice to be mailed shall be a duplicate of the one published in the newspaper, but need not necessarily be a copy of the newspaper itself.

SO ORDERED this _____ day of _____, _____

_____
JUDGE,   SUPERIOR COURT

RETURN OF SERVICE

STATE OF GEORGIA
COUNTY OF _____

I hereby certify that I have published a Notice in the manner and form prescribed in the foregoing Order, and that I have enclosed, directed, stamped and mailed a copy of the said Notice together with a copy of the Order for Service by Publication and Complaint (if any), to _____
_____
This the _____ day of _____, _____.

_____
DEPUTY CLERK
Clerk of Superior Court

ORDER PERFECTING SERVICE

STATE OF GEORGIA
COUNTY OF _____

It appearing to the Court that service upon _____
has been perfected by publication of notice on the _____ day of _____, _____,
and on _____ days of _____ 199____ in the _____,
and by enclosing, directing, stamping, and mailing a copy of the notice together with a copy of the Order for Publication and the Complaint (if any) to said defendant at (his) (her) last known address, and by entry on said case of the actions by the clerk.

IT IS HEREBY ORDERED that said service by publication be, and is approved.

_____
JUDGE,   SUPERIOR COURT

PUBLICATION DATES OK: This the_____ day of _____, _____.

_____
DEPUTY CLERK
Clerk of Superior Court

IN THE SUPERIOR COURT OF _____ **COUNTY**
STATE OF GEORGIA

_____   CIVIL ACTION #_____

PLAINTIFF

VS.

_____

DEFENDANT

TO:

NOTICE OF PUBLICATION

By **ORDER** of the Court for service by publication dated _____,
You are hereby notified that o_____, The above-named
Plaintiff filed suit against you for:

_____.

You are required to file with the Clerk of the Superior Court, and to serve upon the plaintiff's attorney whose name and address is: _____

_____

_____

_____ an
Answer in writing within sixty (60) days of _____.

Witness the Honorable _____, Judge of the
_____ Superior Court.

This the _____ day of _____, _____.

, Clerk

by:

_____
Deputy Clerk of Superior Court

IN THE SUPERIOR COURT OF _____ COUNTY

STATE OF GEORGIA

_____
Plaintiff

CIVIL ACTION

vs.

FILE #:_____

_____
Defendant

AFFIDAVIT OF INDIGENCE

Pursuant to OCGA § 9-15-2, the undersigned swears under oath that because of indigence the undersigned is unable to pay the costs associated with filing of pleadings in this case and prays to be relieved from said costs.

This _____, _____

_____
Affiant

Sworn to and subscribed before me

this _____, _____

Name _____

Address _____

_____

Telephone _____

_____
Notary Public

IN THE SUPERIOR COURT OF _____ COUNTY
STATE OF GEORGIA

_____
Plaintiff

CIVIL ACTION

vs.

FILE #:_____

_____
Defendant

ACKNOWLEDGMENT OF SERVICE AND CONSENT TO JURISDICTION

Comes now _____, Defendant in the above-styled action, who hereby acknowledges service of the above and foregoing Petition for Divorce, consents to the jurisdiction of this Court, and waives notice of further hearings on the within and foregoing matter.

This _____ day of _____, _____.

_____
Defendant

Sworn and subscribed before me
this ____ day of _____, _____.

_____
Notary Public

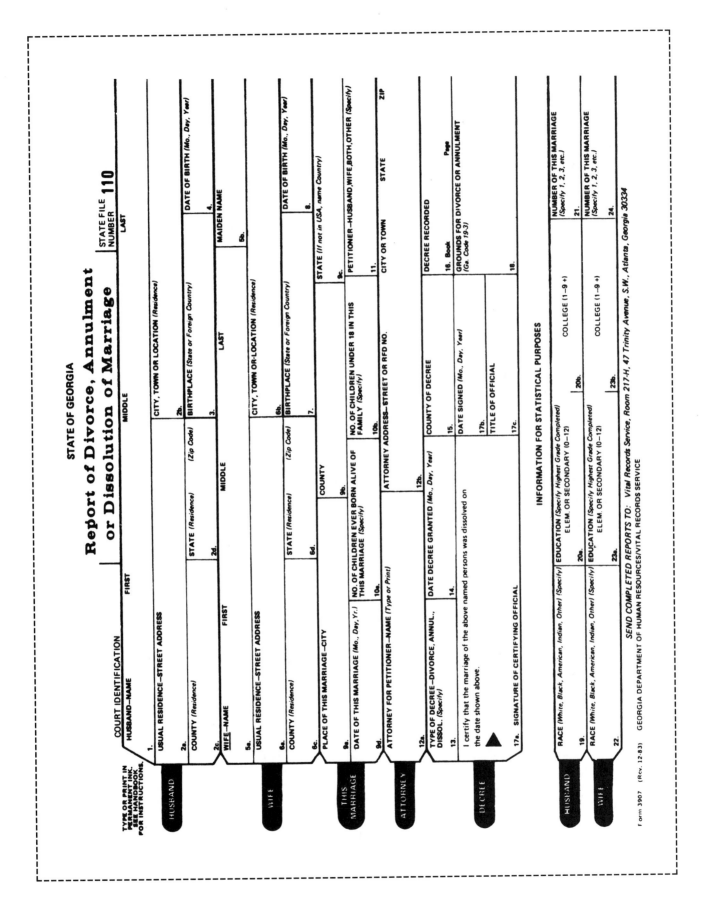

_____ NO. _____

VERSUS

SUPERIOR COURT
_____ COUNTY, GEORGIA

_____

TEMPORARY ORDER

Upon consideration of this case, upon evidence submitted as provided by law, it is the temporary order of the Court that, during the pendency of this action:

IT IS ADJUDGED THAT:

❏ 1. The parties shall share parenting responsibilities; however, physical custody of the minor child(ren) of the parties shall be awarded to the party designated below:

<u>Name of Child</u>   <u>Birthdate</u>   <u>Custody Awarded To:</u>

Each party shall have the right to visit any child not in his or her physical custody at reasonable times and places after reasonable notice to the custodial party.

❏ 2. The ❏ Husband ❏ Wife shall pay temporary child support to the other party in the sum of $ _____ per _____, beginning _____, _____.

❏ 3. The ❏ Husband ❏ Wife shall provide health insurance coverage for the minor child(ren) whenever such insurance is reasonably available.

❏ 4. The ❏ Husband ❏ Wife shall pay temporary alimony to the other party in the sum of $ _____ per _____, beginning _____, _____, until further order of this court.

❑ 5. The ❑ Husband ❑ Wife shall pay the other party's attorney's fees, set at $ _____ (to be paid to _____), and court costs, taxed at $ _____, both of which shall be paid within _____ days of the date of this order.

❑ 6. Other provisions:

ORDERED this _____ day of _____, _____

_____

Judge, Superior Court
County, Georgia

IN THE SUPERIOR COURT OF _____ **COUNTY**
STATE OF GEORGIA

_____

                    Plaintiff   CIVIL ACTION

        vs.   FILE #:_____

_____

                    Defendant

INCOME DEDUCTION ORDER

This Court, having entered an order on _____ *{date}* identifying an obligation of support on behalf of the Plaintiff/Defendant *{cross out whichever does not apply}* in favor of the Plaintiff/Defendant *{cross out whichever does not apply}*, and the Court having been provided the within and foregoing Income Deduction Order at the request of the Plaintiff/Defendant *{cross out whichever does not apply}* and it having been determined that an Income Deduction Order was applicable thereto, in accord with OCGA § 19-6-32, *et seq.*,

IT IS THEREFORE ORDERED AND ADJUDGED

1. INCOME DEDUCTION

That the Plaintiff's/Defendant's *{cross out whichever does not apply}* employer, future employer, or any other person, private entity, federal or state government, or any unit of local government providing or administering income due the Plaintiff/Defendant *{cross out whichever does not apply}* as wage shall deduct from all monies due and payable to the Plaintiff/Defendant *{cross out whichever does not apply}* current support in the amount of $_____ *{amount}* to be deducted in approximate equal amounts each and every pay period during the month, and

2. PLACE OF PAYMENT

The employer shall make the amounts deducted payable to, and forward them within two business days after each payment date to _____ *{name of receiving spouse}*.

3. CONSUMER CREDIT PROTECTION ACT

The maximum amount to be deducted shall not exceed the amounts allowed under 303(b) of the Consumer Credit Protection Act, 15 U.S.C. § 1673(b) as amended.

4. EFFECTIVE DATE

This income deduction order shall be effective immediately.

5. DURATION

This income deduction order supersedes any income deduction order which may have been previously entered in this case. This income deduction order will remain in full force and effect until modified, suspended, or terminated by further Order of this Court. This Order and all further papers required to be served pursuant to OCGA § 19-6-33 shall be served upon the employer by regular first class mail.

DECREE ENTERED, this _____ day of _____, _____.

_____
JUDGE, _____*{county}* Superior Court

Submitted by:

_____

IN THE SUPERIOR COURT OF _____ COUNTY
STATE OF GEORGIA

_____

                   Plaintiff   CIVIL ACTION

     vs.   FILE #:_____

_____

                  Defendant

NOTICE TO PAYOR

To: Human Resources Department

      _____

      _____

      {Employer of paying spouse}

Pursuant to OCGA § 19-6-33 the Payor is hereby notified:

1)   That the payor is hereby required to deduct $_____ *{amount}* of Plaintiff's/Defendant's *{cross out whichever does not apply}* gross income and that amount is to be paid to _____
_____ *{name and address of receiving spouse}*. The amount actually deducted plus all administrative charges shall not be in excess of the amount allowed under Section 303(b) of the Federal Consumer Credit Protection Act, 15 U.S.C. § 1673(b);

2)   That the payor is to implement the income deductin order no later than the first pay period that occurs after 14 days following the date the notice was mailed;

3)   That the payor is to forward to within two business days after each payment date to _____
{name and address of receiving spouse} the amount deducted from _____
_____'s *{paying spouse}* income and a statement as to whether

that amount totally or partially satisfies the periodic amount specified in the income deduction order.

4) That if a payor willfully fails to deduct the proper amount from _____'s *{paying spouse}* income, the payor is liable for the amount the payor should have deducted, plus costs, interest, and reasonable attorney fees;

5) That the payor may collect up to $25.00 against _____'s *{paying spouse}* income to reimburse the payor for administrative costs for the first income deduction order and up to $3.00 for each deduction thereafter;

6) That the income deduction order and the notice to payor are binding on the payor until further notice by obligee or the court or until the payor no longer provides income to the obligor;

7) That when the payor no longer provides income to _____ *{paying spouse}* the payor shall notify _____ *{receiving spouse}* and shall also provide _____'s *{paying spouse}* last known address and the name and address of _____'s *{paying spouse}* new payor, if known, and that, if the payor willfully violates this provision, the payor is subject to a civil penalty not to exceed $250.00 for the first violation or $500.00 for any subsequent violation. Penalties shall be paid to _____ *{receiving spouse}*.

8) That no payor may discharge an obligor by reason of the fact that income has been subject to an income deduction order under Code Section 19-6-32 and that violation of this provision subjects the payor to a civil penalty not to exceed $250.00 for the first violation or $500.00 for a subsequent violation. Penalties will be paid to _____ _____ *{receiving spouse}*. If no support is owing the penalty shall be paid to the obligor.

9) That the income deduction order has priority over all other legal processes under state law pertaining to the same income and that payment as required by the income deduction order is a complete defense by the payor against any claims of the obligor or his creditors as to the sum paid.

10) That if the payor received income deduction orders requiring that the income of two or more obligors be deducted and sent to the same depository he may combine the

amounts paid to the depository in a single payment as long as he identifies that portion of the payment attributable to each obligor.

11)   If payor receives income deduction orders against the same obligor he shall contact the court for further instructions. Upon being contacted the court shall allocate amounts available for income deduction giving priority to current child support obligations up to the limits imposed under Section 303(b) of the Federal Consumer Credit Protection Act, 15 U.S.C. § 1673(b).

DECREE ENTERED this _____ day of _____, _____.

_____

JUDGE, _____ {county} Superior Court

Submitted by:

_____

IN THE SUPERIOR COURT OF _____ COUNTY
STATE OF GEORGIA

_____

Plaintiff   CIVIL ACTION

vs.   FILE #:_____

_____

Defendant

PETITION FOR FAMILY VIOLENCE PROTECTION

Comes now the Plaintiff/Defendant *{cross out whichever does not apply}*, _____ *{victim's name}*, who petitions this Court for protection from domestic violence under the provisions of OCGA § 19-13-1 (The Family Violence Act), showing to the Court the following:

1.

Plaintiff/Defendant *{cross out whichever does not apply}*, _____ *{victim's name}*, has been a resident of the State of Georgia for more than six months immediately preceding the filing of this action.

2.

Plaintiff/Defendant *{cross out whichever does not apply}*, _____ *{offender's name}*, is a resident of the state of Georgia, County of _____ *{county}*, and may be served with process at his/her *{cross out whichever does not apply}* present residence, to wit: _____ *{offender's address}*, and is subject to the jurisdiction and venue of this Court.

3.

On or about _____ {date}, _____

_____

_____

_____

_____ {write down what happened}.

4.

On or about _____ {date}, _____

_____

_____

_____ {write down whether there is any history of violence}.

5.

Plaintiff/Defendant {cross out whichever does not apply}, _____
{victim's name}, is in fear of his/her {cross out whichever does not apply} personal safety and seeks the eviction of the Plaintiff/Defendant {cross out whichever does not apply} from the marital residence, temporary custody of the _____ {number of children} minor child(ren), temporary support, temporary possession of the marital residence, and order preventing and distraining any transfers of marital assets until a complete resolution of this matter is effected.

Wherefore Plaintiff/Defendant {cross out whichever does not apply} seeks the above referenced relief and such other relief as this Court deems appropriate under the circumstances.

This _____ day of _____, _____.

_____

_____
{victim's name}

IN THE SUPERIOR COURT OF _____ **COUNTY**

STATE OF GEORGIA

_____

Plaintiff   CIVIL ACTION

vs.   FILE #:_____

_____

Defendant

VERIFICATION

PERSONALLY appeared before the undersigned attesting officer authorized by law to administer oaths, _____ *{victim's name}*, who, being first duly sworn on oath, deposes and says that the facts alleged in the above and foregoing Petition for Family Violence Protection are true and correct.

_____

_____ *{victim's name}*

Sworn to and subscribed before me this

_____ day of _____, _____.

_____

Notary Public

INDEX

Your #1 Source for Real World Legal Information...

SPHINX® PUBLISHING
A Division of Sourcebooks, Inc.®

- Written by lawyers
- Simple English explanation of the law
- Forms and instructions included

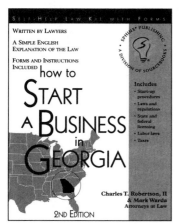

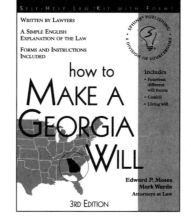

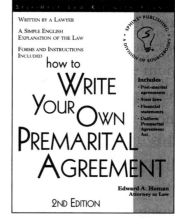

HOW TO START A BUSINESS IN GEORGIA

For anyone starting a business, this book provides essential information on matters crucial to business success, such as: licensing, name registration, worker's compensation, tax laws, and advertising rules. Includes Georgia and Federal forms.

140 pages; $16.95;
ISBN 1-57248-076-9

HOW TO MAKE A GEORGIA WILL 3RD ED.

Without a will, probate laws decide what happens to your property upon death. This book explains Georgia law regarding wills, inheritance, guardianship of children, and joint property. It includes ready-to-use forms, including a living will.

96 pages; $12.95;
ISBN 157248-075-0

HOW TO WRITE YOUR OWN PREMARITAL AGREEMENT, 2ND. ED.

With a divorce reare of over 50 percent, although unpleassant, it is wise to consider drafting your own premarital agreement. Witht his book, you can also cancel or modify an existing premarital agreement.

150 pages; $19.95;
ISBN 1-57071-334-8

See the following order form for books written specifically for California, Florida, Georgia, Illinois, Massachusetts, Michigan, Minnesota, New York, North Carolina, Pennsylvania, and Texas! *Coming soon—Ohio and New Jersey!*

What our customers say about our books:

"It couldn't be more clear for the lay person." —R.D.

"I want you to know I really appreciate your book. It has saved me a lot of time and money." —L.T.

"Your real estate contracts book has saved me nearly $12,000.00 in closing costs over the past year." —A.B.

"...many of the legal questions that I have had over the years were answered clearly and concisely through your plain English interpretation of the law." —C.E.H.

"If there weren't people out there like you I'd be lost. You have the best books of this type out there." —S.B.

"...your forms and directions are easy to follow." —C.V.M.

Sphinx Publishing's Legal Survival Guides
are directly available from the Sourcebooks, Inc., or from your local bookstores.
For credit card orders call 1–800–43–BRIGHT, write P.O. Box 372, Naperville, IL 60566,
or fax 630-961-2168

SPHINX® PUBLISHING'S NATIONAL TITLES

Valid in All 50 States

LEGAL SURVIVAL IN BUSINESS

How to Form a Limited Liability Company	$19.95
How to Form Your Own Corporation (2E)	$19.95
How to Form Your Own Partnership	$19.95
How to Register Your Own Copyright (2E)	$19.95
How to Register Your Own Trademark (3E)	$19.95
Most Valuable Business Legal Forms You'll Ever Need (2E)	$19.95
Most Valuable Corporate Forms You'll Ever Need (2E)	$24.95
Software Law (with diskette)	$29.95

LEGAL SURVIVAL IN COURT

Crime Victim's Guide to Justice	$19.95
Debtors' Rights (3E)	$12.95
Defend Yourself against Criminal Charges	$19.95
Grandparents' Rights (2E)	$19.95
Help Your Lawyer Win Your Case (2E)	$12.95
Jurors' Rights (2E)	$9.95
Legal Malpractice and Other Claims against Your Lawyer (2E)	$18.95
Legal Research Made Easy (2E)	$14.95
Simple Ways to Protect Yourself from Lawsuits	$24.95
Victims' Rights	$12.95
Winning Your Personal Injury Claim	$19.95

LEGAL SURVIVAL IN REAL ESTATE

How to Buy a Condominium or Townhome	$16.95
How to Negotiate Real Estate Contracts (3E)	$16.95
How to Negotiate Real Estate Leases (3E)	$16.95
Successful Real Estate Brokerage Management	$19.95

LEGAL SURVIVAL IN PERSONAL AFFAIRS

Your Right to Child Custody, Visitation and Support	$19.95
The Nanny and Domestic Help Legal Kit	$19.95
How to File Your Own Bankruptcy (4E)	$19.95
How to File Your Own Divorce (3E)	$19.95
How to Make Your Own Will	$12.95
How to Write Your Own Living Will	$9.95
How to Write Your Own Premarital Agreement (2E)	$19.95
How to Win Your Unemployment Compensation Claim	$19.95
Living Trusts and Simple Ways to Avoid Probate (2E)	$19.95
Neighbor v. Neighbor (2E)	$12.95
The Power of Attorney Handbook (3E)	$19.95
Simple Ways to Protect Yourself from Lawsuits	$24.95
Social Security Benefits Handbook (2E)	$14.95
Unmarried Parents' Rights	$19.95
U.S.A. Immigration Guide (3E)	$19.95
Guia de Inmigracion a Estados Unidos (2E)	$19.95

Legal Survival Guides are directly available from Sourcebooks, Inc., or from your local bookstores.

For credit card orders call 1–800–43–BRIGHT, write P.O. Box 372, Naperville, IL 60566,
or fax 630-961-2168

Legal Survival Guides™ State Titles
Up-to-date for Your State

California

How to File for Divorce in CA	$19.95
How to Make a CA Will	$12.95
How to Start a Business in CA	$16.95
How to Win in Small Claims Court in CA	$14.95
Landlords' Rights and Duties in CA	$19.95
CA Power of Attorney Handbook	$19.95

Florida

Florida Power of Attorney Handbook	$9.95
How to Change Your Name in FL (3E)	$14.95
How to File a FL Construction Lien (2E)	$19.95
How to File a Guardianship in FL	$19.95
How to File for Divorce in FL (4E)	$21.95
How to Form a Nonprofit Corp in FL (3E)	$19.95
How to Form a Simple Corp in FL (3E)	$19.95
How to Make a FL Will (5E)	$12.95
How to Modify Your FL Divorce Judgement (3E)	$22.95
How to Probate an Estate in FL (2E)	$24.95
How to Start a Business in FL (4E)	$16.95
How to Win in Small Claims Court in FL (6E)	$14.95
Land Trusts in FL (5E)	$24.95
Landlords' Rights and Duties in FL (7E)	$19.95
Women's Legal Rights in FL	$19.95

Georgia

How to File for Divorce in GA (2E)	$19.95
How to Make a GA Will (2E)	$9.95
How to Start and Run a GA Business (2E)	$18.95

Illinois

How to File for Divorce in IL	$19.95
How to Make an IL Will	$9.95
How to Start a Business in IL	$16.95

Massachusetts

How to File for Divorce in MA (2E)	$19.95
How to Make a MA Will	$9.95
How to Probate an Estate in MA	$19.95
How to Start a Business in MA	$16.95
Landlords' Rights and Duties in MA	$19.95

Michigan

How to File for Divorce in MI	$19.95
How to Make a MI Will	$9.95
How to Start a Business in MI	$16.95

Minnesota

How to File for Divorce in MN	$19.95
How to Form a Simple Corporation in MN	$19.95
How to Make a MN Will	$9.95
How to Start a Business in MN	$16.95

New York

How to File for Divorce in NY	$19.95
How to Make a NY Will	$12.95
How to Start a Business in NY	$16.95
How to Win in Small Claims Court in NY	$14.95
Landlords' Rights and Duties in NY	$19.95
New York Power of Attorney Handbook	$12.95

North Carolina

How to File for Divorce in NC (2E)	$19.95
How to Make a NC Will (2E)	$9.95
How to Start a Business in NC	$16.95

Pennsylvania

How to File for Divorce in PA	$19.95
How to Make a PA Will	$12.95
How to Start a Business in PA	$16.95
Landlords' Rights and Duties in PA	$19.95

Texas

How to File for Divorce in TX (2E)	$19.95
How to Form a Simple Corporation in TX	$19.95
How to Make a TX Will	$9.95
How to Probate an Estate in TX	$19.95
How to Start a Business in TX	$16.95
How to Win in Small Claims Court in TX	$14.95
Landlords' Rights and Duties in TX	$19.95

Legal Survival Guides are directly available from the publisher, or from your local bookstores.

For credit card orders call 1–800–43–BRIGHT, write P.O. Box 372, Naperville, IL 60566, or fax 630-961-2168

SPHINX® PUBLISHING ORDER FORM

Qty	ISBN	Title	Retail	Ext.
		SPHINX PUBLISHING NATIONAL TITLES		
	1-57071-166-6	Crime Victim's Guide to Justice	$19.95	
	1-57071-342-1	Debtors' Rights (3E)	$12.95	
	1-57071-162-3	Defend Yourself against Criminal Charges	$19.95	
	1-57248-082-3	Grandparents' Rights (2E)	$19.95	
	1-57248-087-4	Guia de Inmigracion a Estados Unidos (2E)	$19.95	
	1-57248-103-X	Help Your Lawyer Win Your Case (2E)	$12.95	
	1-57071-164-X	How to Buy a Condominium or Townhome	$16.95	
	1-57071-223-9	How to File Your Own Bankruptcy (4E)	$19.95	
	1-57071-224-7	How to File Your Own Divorce (3E)	$19.95	
	1-57248-083-1	How to Form a Limited Liability Company	$19.95	
	1-57248-099-8	How to Form a Nonprofit Corporation	$24.95	
	1-57071-227-1	How to Form Your Own Corporation (2E)	$19.95	
	1-57071-343-X	How to Form Your Own Partnership	$19.95	
	1-57071-228-X	How to Make Your Own Will	$12.95	
	1-57071-331-6	How to Negotiate Real Estate Contracts (3E)	$16.95	
	1-57071-332-4	How to Negotiate Real Estate Leases (3E)	$16.95	
	1-57071-225-5	How to Register Your Own Copyright (2E)	$19.95	
	1-57248-104-8	How to Register Your Own Trademark (3E)	$19.95	
	1-57071-349-9	How to Win Your Unemployment Compensation Claim	$19.95	
	1-57071-167-4	How to Write Your Own Living Will	$9.95	
	1-57071-344-8	How to Write Your Own Premarital Agreement (2E)	$19.95	
	1-57071-333-2	Jurors' Rights (2E)	$9.95	
	1-57248-032-7	Legal Malpractice and Other Claims against...	$18.95	
	1-57071-400-2	Legal Research Made Easy (2E)	$14.95	
	1-57071-336-7	Living Trusts and Simple Ways to Avoid Probate (2E)	$19.95	
	1-57071-345-6	Most Valuable Bus. Legal Forms You'll Ever Need (2E)	$19.95	
	1-57071-346-4	Most Valuable Corporate Forms You'll Ever Need (2E)	$24.95	
	1-57248-089-0	Neighbor v. Neighbor (2E)	$12.95	
	1-57071-348-0	The Power of Attorney Handbook (3E)	$19.95	
	1-57248-020-3	Simple Ways to Protect Yourself from Lawsuits	$24.95	
	1-57071-337-5	Social Security Benefits Handbook (2E)	$14.95	
	1-57071-163-1	Software Law (w/diskette)	$29.95	
	0-913825-86-7	Successful Real Estate Brokerage Mgmt.	$19.95	
	1-57248-098-X	The Nanny and Domestic Help Legal Kit	$19.95	
	1-57071-399-5	Unmarried Parents' Rights	$19.95	
	1-57071-354-5	U.S.A. Immigration Guide (3E)	$19.95	
	0-913825-82-4	Victims' Rights	$12.95	
	1-57071-165-8	Winning Your Personal Injury Claim	$19.95	
	1-57248-097-1	Your Right to Child Custody, Visitation and Support	$19.95	
		CALIFORNIA TITLES		
	1-57071-360-X	CA Power of Attorney Handbook	$12.95	
	1-57071-355-3	How to File for Divorce in CA	$19.95	
	1-57071-356-1	How to Make a CA Will	$12.95	
	1-57071-408-8	How to Probate an Estate in CA	$19.95	
	1-57071-357-X	How to Start a Business in CA	$16.95	
	1-57071-358-8	How to Win in Small Claims Court in CA	$14.95	
	1-57071-359-6	Landlords' Rights and Duties in CA	$19.95	
		NEW YORK TITLES		
	1-57071-184-4	How to File for Divorce in NY	$19.95	
		FLORIDA TITLES		
	1-57071-363-4	Florida Power of Attorney Handbook (2E)	$12.95	
	1-57248-093-9	How to File for Divorce in FL (6E)	$21.95	
	1-57248-086-6	How to Form a Limited Liability Co. in FL	$19.95	
	1-57071-401-0	How to Form a Partnership in FL	$19.95	
	1-57071-380-4	How to Form a Corporation in FL (4E)	$19.95	
	1-57071-361-8	How to Make a FL Will (5E)	$12.95	
	1-57248-088-2	How to Modify Your FL Divorce Judgment (4E)	$22.95	

Form Continued on Following Page   **SUBTOTAL**

SPHINX® PUBLISHING ORDER FORM

Qty	ISBN	Title	Retail	Ext.
		FLORIDA TITLES (CONT'D)		
____	1-57071-364-2	How to Probate an Estate in FL (3E)	$24.95	____
____	1-57248-081-5	How to Start a Business in FL (5E)	$16.95	____
____	1-57071-362-6	How to Win in Small Claims Court in FL (6E)	$14.95	____
____	1-57071-335-9	Landlords' Rights and Duties in FL (7E)	$19.95	____
____	1-57071-334-0	Land Trusts in FL (5E)	$24.95	____
____	0-913825-73-5	Women's Legal Rights in FL	$19.95	____
		GEORGIA TITLES		
____	1-57071-376-6	How to File for Divorce in GA (3E)	$19.95	____
____	1-57248-075-0	How to Make a GA Will (3E)	$12.95	____
____	1-57248-076-9	How to Start a Business in Georgia (3E)	$16.95	____
		ILLINOIS TITLES		
____	1-57071-405-3	How to File for Divorce in IL (2E)	$19.95	____
____	1-57071-415-0	How to Make an IL Will (2E)	$12.95	____
____	1-57071-416-9	How to Start a Business in IL (2E)	$16.95	____
____	1-57248-078-5	Landlords' Rights & Duties in IL	$19.95	____
		MASSACHUSETTS TITLES		
____	1-57071-329-4	How to File for Divorce in MA (2E)	$19.95	____
____	1-57248-108-0	How to Make a MA Will (2E)	$12.95	____
____	1-57248-109-9	How to Probate an Estate in MA (2E)	$19.95	____
____	1-57248-106-4	How to Start a Business in MA (2E)	$16.95	____
____	1-57248-107-2	Landlords' Rights and Duties in MA (2E)	$19.95	____
		MICHIGAN TITLES		
____	1-57071-409-6	How to File for Divorce in MI (2E)	$19.95	____
____	1-57248-077-7	How to Make a MI Will (2E)	$12.95	____
____	1-57071-407-X	How to Start a Business in MI (2E)	$16.95	____
		MINNESOTA TITLES		
____	1-57248-039-4	How to File for Divorce in MN	$19.95	____
____	1-57248-040-8	How to Form a Simple Corporation in MN	$19.95	____
____	1-57248-037-8	How to Make a MN Will	$9.95	____
____	1-57248-038-6	How to Start a Business in MN	$16.95	____
		NEVADA TITLES		
____	1-57248-101-3	How to Form a Corporation in NV	$19.95	____
		NEW YORK TITLES		
____	1-57071-184-4	How to File for Divorce in NY	$19.95	____

Qty	ISBN	Title	Retail	Ext.
____	1-57248-105-6	How to Form a Corporation in NY	$19.95	____
____	1-57248-095-5	How to Make a NY Will (2E)	$12.95	____
____	1-57071-185-2	How to Start a Business in NY	$16.95	____
____	1-57071-187-9	How to Win in Small Claims Court in NY	$14.95	____
____	1-57071-186-0	Landlords' Rights and Duties in NY	$19.95	____
____	1-57071-188-7	New York Power of Attorney Handbook	$19.95	____
		NORTH CAROLINA TITLES		
____	1-57071-326-X	How to File for Divorce in NC (2E)	$19.95	____
____	1-57071-327-8	How to Make a NC Will (2E)	$12.95	____
____	1-57248-096-3	How to Start a Business in NC (2E)	$16.95	____
____	1-57248-091-2	Landlords' Rights & Duties in NC	$19.95	____
		OHIO TITLES		
____	1-57248-102-1	How to File for Divorce in OH	$19.95	____
		PENNSYLVANIA TITLES		
____	1-57071-177-1	How to File for Divorce in PA	$19.95	____
____	1-57248-094-7	How to Make a PA Will (2E)	$12.95	____
____	1-57248-112-9	How to Start a Business in PA (2E)	$16.95	____
____	1-57071-179-8	Landlords' Rights and Duties in PA	$19.95	____
		TEXAS TITLES		
____	1-57071-330-8	How to File for Divorce in TX (2E)	$19.95	____
____	1-57248-009-2	How to Form a Simple Corporation in TX	$19.95	____
____	1-57071-417-7	How to Make a TX Will (2E)	$12.95	____
____	1-57071-418-5	How to Probate an Estate in TX (2E)	$19.95	____
____	1-57071-365-0	How to Start a Business in TX (2E)	$16.95	____
____	1-57248-111-0	How to Win in Small Claims Court in TX (2E)	$14.95	____
____	1-57248-110-2	Landlords' Rights and Duties in TX (2E)	$19.95	____

SUBTOTAL THIS PAGE ____

SUBTOTAL PREVIOUS PAGE ____

Illinois residents add 6.75% sales tax
Florida residents add 6% state sales tax plus applicable discretionary surtax ____

Shipping— $4.00 for 1st book, $1.00 each additional ____

TOTAL ____